The Dream of Prosperity in Colonial America

Anson G. Phelps Lectureship on Early American History

✱

Charles M. Andrews, OUR EARLIEST COLONIAL SETTLEMENTS: THEIR
DIVERSITIES OF ORIGINS AND LATER CHARACTERISTICS

Carl Bridenbaugh, THE COLONIAL CRAFTSMAN

Wesley Frank Craven, THE LEGEND OF THE FOUNDING FATHERS

Dixon Ryan Fox, YANKEES AND YORKERS

Evarts B. Greene, RELIGION AND THE STATE: THE MAKING AND TESTING OF
AN AMERICAN TRADITION

Leonard W. Labaree, CONSERVATISM IN EARLY AMERICAN HISTORY

Andrew C. McLaughlin, THE FOUNDATIONS OF AMERICAN
CONSTITUTIONALISM

Samuel Eliot Morison, THE PURITAN PRONAOS: STUDIES IN THE
INTELLECTUAL LIFE OF NEW ENGLAND IN THE SEVENTEENTH
CENTURY
[Revised and retitled THE INTELLECTUAL LIFE OF COLONIAL NEW
ENGLAND]

D. Plooij, THE PILGRIM FATHERS FROM A DUTCH POINT OF VIEW

Richard Harrison Shryock, MEDICINE AND SOCIETY IN AMERICA 1660–1860

Thomas J. Wertenbaker, THE GOLDEN AGE OF COLONIAL CULTURE

The Dream of Prosperity
in Colonial America

*
---
*

LOUIS B. WRIGHT

NEW YORK UNIVERSITY PRESS · 1965

Preface

THE four chapters in this volume are printed as they were delivered. No effort has been made to alter the lecture form. They are a part of a longer projected study of social and economic influences that affected the development of the English colonies in North America.

The author wishes to express his profound appreciation of the hospitality and courtesies shown him by the authorities of New York University, particularly President James M. Hester, Dr. Thomas P. Robinson, vice-president, Professor Bayrd Still, chairman of the history department, and Professor Brooke Hindle.

In the preparation of the lectures, he owes a continuing debt to Miss Virginia LaMar, Mrs. Elaine Fowler, Mrs. John Hendrickson, and Mrs. William Leonard of the Folger research and editorial staffs.

LOUIS B. WRIGHT

The Folger Library
March 19, 1964

Contents

Preface   v

I
American Cornucopia for All the World   1

II
The Lure of Fish, Furs, Wine, and Silk   21

III
Cures for All the Ills of Mankind   41

IV
The Continuing Dream of an Economic Utopia   63

Index   91

I

American Cornucopia for All the World

FOR nearly five hundred years Europeans have looked across the Atlantic and dreamed of an infinite variety of benefits that might accrue to them from the wealth of the new world. The American taxpayer in the 1960's is acutely aware of an almost universal faith in the American cornucopia—a horn of plenty that continually pours out dollars or the equivalent in commodities for the salvation of less prosperous or less provident peoples. This concept of an ever-flowing cornucopia is as old as the discovery of America, and in one fashion or another it has affected the course of history since 1492. It helps to explain the attitudes of immigrants to the new world and many aspects of colonial development. In the light of the continuing belief in the material benefits still obtainable from North America, a fresh survey of the genesis of these ideas may be useful and enlightening.

Europe in 1492 was poised between two eras: the Middle Ages, with a legacy of emphasis upon ecclesiastical authority and religious devotion, and the modern age, only faintly visible as yet but already showing a tendency toward secularism and a new emphasis upon material things. During the later Middle Ages, western Europeans had gradually acquired a taste for luxuries. The Crusaders had learned through contacts with Greek Byzantines, with merchants in Alexandria, and with the Saracens in the Holy Land that Asia held vast stores of good things pleasing to the palates and the vanities of men. Spices, exotic foods, silks, soft cottons, jewels, golden ornaments, fine cutlery, and a variety of other products filtered into Europe. Venice and, later, Genoa grew prosperous on trade with the East, and, despite the age-old hostility between Christian and Moslem, a way of trade developed somewhat analogous to our own contacts with the countries behind the Iron Curtain.

The growth of trade and the exploitation of silver mines in eastern Europe during the fifteenth century put more money into circulation and stimulated an increased demand for the luxuries of Asia. Furthermore, coincidentally with this increasing demand came a curtailment of supplies from Asia caused by the military successes of the Ottoman Turks and a withdrawal of the ruling dynasty in China from contacts with the "foreign devils" whom earlier Mongol rulers had tolerated. Venice and Genoa still managed to bring rich argosies of eastern wares to European markets, but the scarcity of these products was such that merchants were able to charge exorbitant prices.

During the first quarter of the fifteenth century, Portugal developed a group of enterprising seamen and merchants who would eventually challenge Venetian supremacy in the eastern trade. Prince Henry of Portugal established in 1416 at Sagres a famous school for navigators, and for this effort he has been known to English historians as "Prince Henry the Navigator." To this school he welcomed seamen from all nations and enlisted them in the service of Portugal. They would soon be probing the Western Ocean and exploring the coastline of Africa. Daring pilots trained by Portugal sometimes took service with other nations. They were free agents, somewhat like the *condottieri* of Italy, ready to sell their talents to the highest bidders. Some of the pilots in the exploring expeditions sent out later by England were Portuguese. Ferdinand Magellan, who made the first circumnavigation of the globe, was a Portuguese, but he sailed under the flag of Spain. Portuguese explorers by the mid-fifteenth century had probed the coast of Africa as far south as Gambia. An Italian in the service of Portugal, one Alvise ça da Mosto, left a notebook in which he described an impossible creature called a hippopotamus and told of eating roast elephant because no other Christian had undergone such an experience.

Tales of the riches of Africa had long circulated in Europe. Readers of the Bible remembered that King Solomon had found on that continent not only the Queen of Sheba but gold and ivory and other precious commodities. The fabulous kingdom of Prester John was supposed to lie somewhere in Africa or Asia. The discoveries of the Portuguese explorers confirmed many of the tales and demonstrated the value of exploiting new territories. Every voyage stirred merchants and traders to make further efforts to obtain the wealth of the East. India was the ultimate objective of the explorers. In 1486–88 Bartholomew Dias sailed around the Cape of Good Hope, made a landing on the east coast of Africa, and returned to report that the way to India was open. Columbus was in Lisbon when Dias got back and made notes concerning his voyage. The belief of Portuguese merchants that profitable contacts with India could be made by sea received final confirmation in 1497–99 when Vasco da Gama reached Calicut and laid the foundation of a Portuguese empire in the East.

A Genoese navigator, Christopher Columbus, got the notion that he could tap the wealth of China, Japan, and the Indies by sailing westward beyond the Canaries. He had read Marco Polo's narrative of his overland journey to China and had seen a map drawn by Toscanelli that convinced him that the circumference of the world was much smaller than it is. To obtain financial backing for his "Enterprise of the Indies," Columbus appealed in vain to crafty King John II of Portugal, to King Henry VII of England, and to Charles VIII of France. For one reason or another, they put him off. At last, as every schoolchild knows, he obtained the necessary support from Ferdinand and Isabella of Spain. They were unwilling to see their neighbor, Portugal, monopolize the trade by sea with the East.

To pious Queen Isabella, Columbus emphasized the virtue of carrying the gospel of Christ to the heathen of Asia. But he also made it clear that this message could be carried at a profit, that the wealth of the fabled East would be theirs, and that no longer need they be beholden to the Venetians or any other sea power. Somewhere across the Western Ocean, Columbus believed, lay the terrestrial paradise, the site of Eden, probably as fertile and propitious as it was when the archangel with his flaming sword drove out sinning Adam and Eve. Columbus stressed the notion of an earthly paradise across the seas, a notion that would take hold of European imaginations for long generations to come, a notion indeed that has not yet completely vanished. One reason for some European bitterness over America in our own time is disappointment because we have not revealed the Eden that, dreamers fancied, ought to be here.

Columbus was convinced that he held the key to the discovery of the good things of the East. He was not seeking a new world, which of course he had no idea existed. He was merely trying to find a new way to the old world, which had wealth uncounted. And when at last on October 12, 1492, he made a landfall in the Bahamas, he thought he had found an island off Japan. Even after four voyages he never understood that he had opened the way to a new world; he died convinced that Cathay lay just beyond the land barrier that blocked the passage of his ships.

In his first voyage Columbus observed that some of the natives wore gold nose plugs and had necklaces of pearl. In November, 1492, he discovered the island we call Cuba, and an exploring party reported that men and women carried firebrands to light the rolled leaves of an herb which they smoked. Gold, pearls, and tobacco would prove immensely profitable to the Spaniards and others who came after them. As yet Columbus did not realize the significance of tobacco, but he set out to find the sources of the gold and pearls.

From this time onward, gold fever would be a dominant motivation of explorers of all nations.

If Columbus did not realize that he had discovered a new continent, he did believe that he had found the terrestrial paradise. On his third voyage, in 1498, he sailed along the coast of Venezuela and became convinced that the country inland from the Gulf of Paria was verily the site of Eden. In a letter describing this portion of his exploration, sent to their majesties King Ferdinand and Queen Isabella, Columbus elaborated his views of the site of Eden. He cited authorities from the past who discussed the problem—St. Isidore, the Venerable Bede, Strabo, St. Ambrose, and Duns Scotus —all of whom agreed that the earthly paradise lay in the East, where Columbus thought he was. He had observed strong currents of fresh water in the Gulf of Paria (from the Orinoco and Rio Grande rivers) and he was certain that these streams of fresh water emanated from the four rivers of paradise, mentioned in Genesis 2:8–15, and familiar to any reader of medieval literature.[1]

"I do not suppose that the Earthly Paradise is in the form of a rugged mountain," he adds for the information of their majesties,

as the descriptions of it have made it appear, but that it is on the summit of the spot which I have described as being in the form of the stalk of a pear. The approach to it from a distance must be by a constant and gradual ascent, but I believe that, as I have already said, no one could ever reach the top. I think also that the water I have described may proceed from it, though it be far off, and that stopping at the place which I have just left [an anchorage in the Gulf of Paria] it forms this lake. There are great indications of this being the Terrestrial Paradise, for its site coincides with the opinion of the holy and wise theologians whom I have mentioned; and, moreover, the other evidences agree with the supposition, for I have never either read or heard of fresh water coming in so large a quantity, in close conjunction with the water of the sea. The idea is also corroborated by the blandness of the temperature; and if the water of which I speak does not proceed from the Earthly Paradise, it seems to be a still greater wonder, for I do not believe that there is any river in the world so large or so deep.[2]

The belief that the earthly paradise actually existed and that men might find it was seriously held by Columbus' age and was not abandoned for many years. This belief was stimulated by a wide variety of literature that flourished in the Middle Ages and continued to circulate. Ultimately it derived from the description in Genesis of the Garden of Eden from which God expelled the first man and woman for eating of the forbidden fruit of the Tree of Knowledge.

The garden motif also flourished in pagan literatures. The Mohammedans believed in an earthly paradise, and Marco Polo in his *Travels* described this Mohammedan garden of pleasures with its pavilions and palaces, streams flowing with wine, milk, and honey, fine ladies, and "the most beautiful damsels in the world who could play on all manner of instruments and sing most sweetly, and danced in a manner charming to behold."[3] Marco Polo's accounts were well known to Columbus and other explorers who might not be averse to finding the Mohammedan paradise because, according to some accounts, the Christian paradise was protected from man's trespass by an inaccessible mountain, or even by a wall of fire.

Not all writers agreed that the earthly paradise, if found, would be forbidden to its discoverers. In some medieval legends, adventurers had stumbled on it and had lived to tell the tale of its wonders: its fruits and flowers, its temperate climate and soft airs, its singing birds, its crystal springs of health-giving waters, its streams with gravel beds of pure gold or pearls, its precious stones including rubies and carbuncles so large that they shone with the light of suns, and its many other marvels that emanated from the imaginations of writers. Some of these wonders were reported as pure facts by pious authors, geographers, and encyclopedists. Other tales of the earthly paradise cropped up in romances that flourished in the Middle Ages and continued in popularity until they turned the giddy brain of Don Quixote.

The significant fact for us is that much of this legend was believed, not only by Columbus and his contemporaries, but by men like Walter Raleigh. As we shall see, they believed that almost anything might be found in the lands across the Atlantic, and nothing was too fantastic to be credited or possible. Even those who feared that God would not allow them to enter the terrestrial paradise, if they found it, believed that there were benefits to be derived from the search. For example, a twelfth-century *Account of Elysaeus* reported that the four rivers of paradise (located on top of four mountains in India) brought down a flood of precious stones and fragrant apples. The mere smell of these apples would heal diseases and relieve hunger and thirst.[4] Though one might not ascend to the top of the mountain, one could harvest the floating apples and dip up bags of precious stones. Romances concerned with the life of Alexander the Great, particularly the *Iter ad Paradisum* (Journey to Paradise), emphasize the precious metals and jewels to be found. This romance also tells of the Well of Life, where Alexander's cook, dipping up water to wash a fish that he was preparing for dinner, was astonished to have the fish come to life. In the later romance of *Huon of Bordeaux,* the hero finds a garden in paradise where there is a fountain of youth: the bottom of the fountain is gravel of pure gold. Another fountain is all of jasper and azure, with flowers of fine gold.[5]

Another widely known medieval story was the *Legend of Seth,* which told of the journey made by Adam's son to the Garden of Eden to bring back the oil of mercy. In an early version of this legend, Seth's mother Eve accompanies him. They fail to get the oil, for the angel guarding the gates of Eden forbids their entry, but they are permitted to bring back spices and drugs: cinnamon, saffron, calamus, and spikenard. The idea that the earthly paradise was the source of spices and curative herbs was firmly implanted in the European consciousness. Since spices and drugs were among the commodities that the East had long supplied, the explorers hoped that the closer they came to the earthly paradise, the greater would be the quantity, variety, and virtue of the spices and herbs to be found. Columbus carried samples of spices and herbs which he exhibited to Indians whom he encountered, but he did not anchor long enough in the Gulf of Paria to see whether the land that he thought was Eden afforded supplies of spices such as Seth had found. Even more unfortunately for Columbus, he did not take time to investigate the source of the pearls that the Indians of "Los Jardines"—the region of the earthly paradise—told him were to be found on the Venezuelan coast behind the island of Margarita. As Professor Morison comments, "A bushel or two of pearls sent home to the Sovereigns would have spoken louder than all the Admiral's description, far more authoritatively than his imaginary discovery of the Terrestrial Paradise." [6] When Columbus returned from the third voyage, one of his former pilots, Alonso de Hojeda, got possession of his charts, made a voyage to the Gulf of Paria, and discovered the pearl fisheries. In 1500 Peralonso Niño obtained there a rich cargo of pearls, and for generations to come Spaniards made fortunes from pearls found on the Venezuelan coast. One voyager observed at low tide half-opened oysters hanging from mango tree roots and declared that these were pearl oysters waiting for the dew drops to fall into them and make pearls. For this was the way early writers accounted for the manufacture of pearls. These riches helped to confirm the belief in the earthly paradise hidden in this newly found land, which many explorers still thought was either an appendage of China or India or very close to them.

One continuing theme that runs through much of the medieval literature on the earthly paradise is the description of a fountain of youth, or a well of life. If Alexander's cook had a fish come to life because he washed it in the water from this magic well, men might also obtain miraculous help from its waters. The best-known search for the fountain of youth was that made by Juan Ponce de León, the explorer of Florida. Historians of Florida like to think that Ponce de León was up to more serious business than looking for a miraculous fountain, but the legend persists and has been of vast service to Florida real estate promoters and advertisers. Modern historians find it difficult to believe that a man capable of conquering and governing Puerto Rico, as Ponce de León had done, would be so gullible as to accept as fact the myth of the fountain of youth and go in search of it, but such historians are oblivious to the literary legacy that Ponce de León had inherited. He had also been a companion of Columbus in his second voyage of 1493, and he must have shared many of his commander's notions. Columbus himself was no less gullible than most of his age in believing in the wonders awaiting discovery, and Ponce de León would have seen nothing fantastic in the stories that he picked up about a fabulous island of Bimini with a fountain and river that renewed the youth of anyone who bathed in it.[7] When he set out from Puerto Rico on March 3, 1513, on his first expedition in search of Bimini, supposed to lie north of Cuba, he had in his consciousness stories of the magic fountain. Gold and slaves, which he had taken in Puerto Rico, had already made him rich. If he should find the fabled fountain of youth, that discovery would add the final benefit to his efforts. What he found was the mainland, where he disembarked about the time of the Easter Feast of Flowers, the *Pascua Florida,* and he named the land "La Florida."

We need not doubt that he looked for the mysterious fountain. Early historians indicate the incentives that motivated Ponce de León's search. Peter Martyr, for example, in his *Decades of the New World,* describing Ponce de León's expedition of 1513, reports an island "in which there is a perennial spring of running water of such marvelous virtue that the water thereof being drunk, perhaps with some diet, makes old men young again." [8] And he provides an example of its specific power. A certain islander, a man "grievously oppressed with old age," drank the waters of this spring which brought to him "manly strength" to such a degree that he "practiced all manly exercises" and "married again and begat children." When Peter Martyr sent his account to Pope Leo X, he warned him not to treat the story lightly. The report had spread throughout the court of Spain, the author added, and "many of them, whom wisdom or fortune has divided from the common sort, think it to be true." Ponce de León was in Spain the year after his first contact with Florida, but he left no account of the expedition himself and we do not know what he told the court about the rejuvenating waters. It was too good a story, however, to deny and, as Peter Martyr comments, many continued to believe it. The fabled island of Bimini persisted in Ponce de León's dreams, for he obtained from the king in 1514 a patent for discovering, colonizing, and governing that island and Florida.

But Florida was not yet destined to become the earthly paradise, with or without the fountain of youth. That development had to wait for the promotional literature of the twentieth century and the ministrations of the subdividers, when lo! they discovered Miami Beach.

In the meantime, one Vasco Núñez de Balboa, a settler on Hispaniola, had made a voyage in 1500 to the coast of Central America and had heard tales of gold and pearls, as well as great stores of food somewhere to the west. In 1510 Balboa, joining an expedition bound for the Venezuelan coast, was instrumental in directing it eventually to settle at Darien on the Isthmus of Panama. Rumors of vast hoards of gold were already rife among the ruthless adventurers who found themselves in Panama. Among these men was one Francisco Pizarro, who would later find gold that eluded others. But at the moment Balboa was planning to discover for himself the treasure that the Indians talked about. His enemies, however, had already carried accusations to Spain of his misdoings and he was threatened with recall to Spain to stand trial. At this juncture he wrote a famous letter to King Ferdinand appealing for a thousand men and supplies to bring back treasure beyond the dreams of avarice. Down the coast to the westward, he has heard, thanks to the favor of God, of great stores of gold. Some of the Indians have so much wealth that they "store their gold in barbacoas like maize, because it is so abundant that they do not care to keep it in baskets; that all the rivers of these mountains contain gold; and they have very large lumps in great abundance." He himself has been very near these mountains but needs additional men to reach them. The Indians report that on the coast of the other sea, three days' journey away, "there are many large pearls, and that the caciques have baskets of them." And he adds for the king's contemplation this thought: "It is a most astonishing thing and without equal that our Lord has made you the lord of this land." [9]

Though the king turned a deaf ear to Balboa's plea, this daring adventurer set out to find the treasure. On September 25, 1513, he reached an eminence near the western coast and climbed to the summit. There on a peak in Darien Balboa got a glimpse of the Pacific Ocean. Down that coast stretched a land whose extent not even the Indians knew, and the people thereof had riches beyond belief. It was not to be Balboa's fortune to reap any reward from his discovery. His enemies ultimately prevailed, and Francisco Pizarro it was who arrested him, conducted him to his trial, and watched while the executioner struck off his head. Twelve years later Pizarro, with his brothers, found and captured the fabulous treasure of the Incas in Peru.

But before the gold of the Incas was a reality to the Spaniards, indeed, in the year that Balboa lost his life, Hernando Cortez reached Tenochtitlán, Montezuma's capital in Mexico, and found that the king of the Aztecs ate from dishes of solid gold, washed in vessels of solid gold, and had even humbler utensils of the precious metal. Here indeed was wealth such as no man had known outside of medieval romances about the earthly paradise. When the Aztecs rose against the invaders on June 20, 1520 (the *noche triste* of the conquerors), many a Spaniard lost his life because the weight of the gold that he was loath to abandon impeded his progress over the causeway.

Not only did the Spaniards find an immense treasure in Central and South America—objects of gold and silver and baskets of pearls—but they located the mines of the precious metals and the fisheries whence came the pearls and enslaved the Indians to produce further wealth for their masters. When this treasure reached Spain—and as the stories of it increased with the telling—all Europe decided that the fables of the earthly paradise had come true. Peter Martyr the historian was convinced that the new lands would produce the spices that were so eagerly sought, and explorers continued to look for the products of the East that Columbus was certain he would find. The notion that the new world was an appendage of China died hard, and for long years into the sixteenth century writers insisted that the Central American coast was the Golden Chersonese, near unto Malaya, where the spices grew.

During the first half of the sixteenth century and even later, the Spaniards maintained a virtual monopoly of the wealth that came from the new world. The Portuguese in the meantime were growing rich on the trade with Africa. Englishmen, Frenchmen, and others looked with envy upon their Iberian neighbors and plotted ways of cutting in upon this golden stream that poured into Spanish and Portuguese ports. The most obvious expedient was to go out upon the high seas and take it, and this was the course followed by many a buccaneer. Englishmen organized syndicates to send out roving expeditions to trade surreptitiously in Portuguese and Spanish territory or to capture such cargoes as they might encounter upon the high seas. Men of high estate took part in these enterprises and Queen Elizabeth herself occasionally lent a royal ship and took a lion's share of the prize money. George Clifford, third Earl of Cumberland, Sir Walter Raleigh, Sir John Hawkins, and Sir Francis Drake are among the best known of the leaders of the Elizabethan corsairs.

The richest single capture was that of the great Portuguese carrack of 1600 tons, the "Madre de Dios," taken in 1592 by a fleet of ten English rovers who eventually brought her into Dartmouth harbor. Ships of Cumberland and Raleigh were chiefly responsible for the capture, but Queen Elizabeth, who had contributed one vessel to the expedition, claimed all the pepper (a very valuable commodity), worth £80,000. The "Madre de Dios" was loaded with all sorts of spices, perfumes, cochineal, silks, brocades, gold, jewelry, and precious stones. Much of this treasure was taken by common sailors and ships' officers before the queen's men could prevent the pillage. Sir Robert Cecil, who went down to Devonshire to see what could be learned about the spoil that disappeared, wrote back to his father, Lord Burghley, that he could smell the sailors who had been aboard the "Madre de Dios" because they had come off loaded with musk and other perfumes.[10] Some seamen, drunk in Dartmouth taverns, pulled from their pockets rubies, diamonds, and pearls by the handful. Others were loaded with gold, and still others staggered off into alleys with sacks of spice on their shoulders. The capture of each new treasure ship from Africa or Asia whetted the appetites of the captors for more and stirred them to try to obtain some portion of the new lands whence came so much wealth.

Of all the Elizabethans, Sir Walter Raleigh made the most persistent and enduring efforts to find and seize for himself and the queen a part of the wealth-producing territory overseas. From the 1580's until his death he dreamed of an English empire in the new world and of the discovery of mines that would make him and his sovereign rich. The story of his attempts at colonization on the coast of North Carolina has been so often told that it needs no repetition, but his entanglement in the legend of an earthly paradise, with its influence upon his activities, is less well known. In Alexander Ross's epitome of Raleigh's *History of the World,* to which he gave the title *The Marrow of History* (1650), occurs a passage summarizing Raleigh's views on this subject. "By what is said," Raleigh declares,

> it appears that Paradise was created a part of this earth and seated in the lower part of Eden or Mesopotamia, containing also a part of Shimr [Shinar?] and Armenia; it stands 35 degrees from the Equinoctial and 55 from the North Pole, in a temperate climate, full of excellent fruits, chiefly of palm trees, without labor; for whereinsoever the earth, nature, and the sun can most vaunt that they have excelled, yet shall the palm tree

be the greater wonder of all their work. This tree alone giveth unto man whatsoever his life beggeth at nature's hand. . . . By how much Adam exceeded all living men in perfection, by being the immediate workmanship of God, by so much did that chosen and particular garden exceed all the parts of the universal world in which God had planted the trees of life and knowledge, plants only proper and belonging to the Paradise and Garden of so great a Lord.[11]

The notion of palm trees being botanical indicators of Paradise was not peculiar to Raleigh. At first sight, some of the early explorers of Florida and South Carolina also thought that the palmetto trees pointed the way to Eden. Bogged down in the mire of the palmetto thickets, they soon reversed their opinions.

By Raleigh's time, of course, no one any longer thought of the new world as a part of Asia, but explorers clung to the hope of finding a passage through the land barrier to the Pacific. The search for a northwest passage would continue for many long years. The idea that the earthly paradise might possibly have had its location, not in Asia at all, but in this new land that God had preserved in a pristine state until in His wisdom He chose to reveal it, gained currency. Even if the new world did not actually contain the site of the original Eden of Genesis, it held areas of Eden-like perfection, and promoters from the sixteenth century until the 1960's have continued that assertion. Promoters have a habit of convincing themselves. That explains nearly every real estate "boom and bust," as can be shown by the history of Florida real estate promotion.

One of the reasons for the failure of some of the early colonial ventures was too great a faith in the productivity and goodness of the new Eden which settlers were about to inhabit. They had been told of a land flowing with milk and honey, where the climate was benign and nature showered a bountiful harvest of good things to sustain life. If they did not immediately discover hoards of gold and pearls to make themselves rich, they would at least find an abundance of food and would be able to live off the land.

Actual contact with the new world soon showed would-be settlers that hard labor, ingenuity, and courage would be required of those who survived. Nature would not automatically take care of them. But the legend of a work-free Eden died hard. The wreck of Sir Thomas Gates's ship the "Sea Venture" in the Bermudas in 1609 and the survival of his party because of the bountiful food and benign climate found there indicated to some Englishmen that, at least in some areas of the new world, Eden existed. Gates had a hard time forcing all of his party to leave for Virginia, and when they finally arrived at Jamestown and found that settlement starving, they looked back upon Bermuda with longing and regret.

Raleigh's explorers, Amadas and Barlow, had given a fine report of the fruitfulness of Virginia (now North Carolina) when they returned, and Raleigh was convinced that he had hit upon a veritable paradise for his colonizing efforts. Furthermore, he was aware that the thirty-fifth parallel of north latitude cut through this territory and that on this parallel Eden was to be found. Surely Virginia would be as goodly a country as Mesopotamia. His spies had found grapes and other tropical fruits, and maybe palms were there too. One could not go wrong with a settlement in such a location. Unhappily, events prevented the realization of Raleigh's dream, but others continued to embroider the theme that this territory would prove a new Eden. A town in North Carolina was later given the very name of Eden, and William Byrd wrote a promotion tract with the title of the "New Found Eden" to persuade Swiss to buy some of his North Carolina land.

Raleigh's capacity to fool himself with the dream of an earthly paradise in the new world shows no credulity unusual in that age. Many others were even harder to convince of the grim realities of settlement overseas and the elusiveness of easy wealth. The legends of the Middle Ages, the apparent confirmation of some of these legends by the Spanish conquests, and the good things that returning travelers reported all made it difficult not to believe any story however fantastic.

Raleigh's own search for the fabled city of Manoa and the wealth of El Dorado somewhere in the drainage system of the Orinoco River illustrates the vitality of the legends that continued to circulate. Raleigh virtually bankrupted himself and eventually went to his execution because of the disasters and failures connected with his last voyage to Guiana in 1617 in search of El Dorado. The cupidity of King James I was sufficient to enable him to forgive Raleigh's hostile encounter with the Spaniards on the Orinoco if he had found the promised gold, but King James could not overlook failure.

The legend of El Dorado, of an Indian king who rolled in gold dust until his body was coated and then washed it off each night in a sacred spring, haunted Spanish and other explorers, who went on numerous expeditions into the interior of South America hoping to find the empire of this gold-encrusted ruler. At length the name of the gilded king was translated to the country itself. El Dorado became a place to be put on the map if only one could find it. The chief city of El Dorado, richer than any yet discovered, was called Manoa.[12]

Hundreds of Spaniards lost their lives looking for this country before Raleigh in the 1590's was infected with the virus of El Dorado. He had obtained information that led him to believe that Manoa, which he equated with El Dorado, lay on the upper reaches of the Orinoco or one of its tributaries. To find that wealth, which would restore him to the favor of Queen Elizabeth, he set out on an expedition to Guiana in February, 1595. Though this first expedition did not find Manoa, Raleigh's faith was undimmed and he returned to write a book about his adventures that contained some elements of the legend of the earthly paradise. The tract bore the enticing title of *The Discoverie Of The Large, Rich, and Bewtiful Empyre Of Guiana, With a relation of the great and Golden Citie of Manoa (which the Spanyards call El Dorado) And of the Prouinces of Emeria, Arromaia, Amapaia, and other Countries, with their riuers, adioyning. Performed in the yeare 1595 by Sir W. Ralegh, Knight.* . . . (1596). "The Empire of Guiana is directly east from Peru towards the sea," he asserts "and lieth vnder the equinoctial line and it hath more abundance of gold than any part of Peru, and as many or more great cities than ever Peru had when it flourished most." [13] Raleigh received reports of drinking bouts of Guiana's emperor and his nobles at which they were all anointed with balsam and thickly powdered with gold. He heard of a crystal mountain whence the Indians gathered diamonds and other precious stones. He also learned about tribes who had their eyes in their shoulders and their mouths in the middle of their breasts, "which though it may be thought a mere fable, yet for mine own part, I am resolved it is true," he adds.[14] This tale goes back to medieval literature and may be found in the fictional travels of Sir John Mandeville. Shakespeare, who probably got it from Raleigh, has Othello tell Desdemona of the sights that he too had seen, of

> The cannibals, that each other eat,
> The anthropophi, and men whose heads
> Do grow beneath their shoulders.

Raleigh was aware of the outlandish nature of this report, and he regretted that he had not heard the exact location of these people until he had left, for, he continues,

> I might have brought one of them with me to put the matter out of doubt. Such a nation was written of by Mandeville, whose reports were held for fables many years and yet since the East Indies were discovered, we find his relations true of such things as heretofore were held incredible.

That anything might be believed about the wonders of the world revealed by recent discovery and exploration, even the accuracy of the fables of Mandeville, Raleigh thus clearly asserts, and others were ready to corroborate his views. No tale in the literature of the Middle Ages about the marvels of the terrestrial paradise, now perhaps discoverable in the new world, was too exaggerated to find some believer. The infinite goodness of the new land was the theme used to lure adventurers and would-be colonists to seek their fortunes overseas for generations after Raleigh's time.

Raleigh's own faith in Guiana led him to seek release from the Tower of London in 1617 to search once more for the land of gold. That voyage resulted in a disastrous encounter with the Spaniards in violation of his promise to the king, the death of his son Wat, and his return to his own death on Tower Hill.

The terrestrial paradise eluded Raleigh as it had eluded thousands before him, but the search did not end with Raleigh, or even with the generation that came after him. In one sense or another, emigrants to the new world were all hopeful of finding some sort of Eden. For those who survived and adapted to conditions in America, the country eventually provided opportunities surpassing any they had known at home. For thousands of others, however, the new world merely proved the gateway to the next world and such hope of paradise as their deserts warranted. Yet, despite disasters, disappointments, and failures suffered by many, North America in the seventeenth and eighteenth centuries remained a dream of goodness to the oppressed of Europe. Literature poured from the press extolling the new Edens that awaited the courageous. Even today the land across the sea continues to beckon to many a beleaguered European, and the bounty of this country appears unlimited to those who have experienced its generosity. Natives on islands in the western Pacific developed a "cargo cult" as the result of food and raiment delivered by American planes in the last war. They confidently expect supplies sent from the American paradise to continue raining from the skies. The dream of the American cornucopia has penetrated to the most distant parts of the earth and thousands predicate their lives on the belief that it will never be empty.

Notes

1. A vast literature throughout the Middle Ages describes the earthly paradise. For a discussion of this literature see Howard R. Patch, *The Other World According to Descriptions in Medieval Literature* (Cambridge, Mass., 1950), *passim*. See also George H. Williams, *Wilderness and Paradise in Christian Thought* (New York, 1962), Josephine Waters Bennett, *The Rediscovery of Sir John Mandeville* (New York, 1954), and Leonardo Olschki, "Ponce de León's Fountain of Youth: History of a Geographical Myth," *Hispanic American Historical Review*, XXI (1941), 361–85. Columbus' knowledge of this background and his concept of the earthly paradise as situated in Venezuela are discussed by Samuel E. Morison, *Admiral of the Ocean Sea: A Life of Columbus* (Boston, 1942), II, 253–93.

2. R. H. Major (ed.), *Select Letters of Christopher Columbus*. Hakluyt Society, 2d ed. (London, 1870), 142–43.

3. Quoted by Patch, *The Other World*, pp. 149, 152, 160.

4. *Ibid.*, pp. 149, 152.

5. *Ibid.*, pp. 157–62.

6. Morison, *Admiral of the Ocean Sea*, II, 278–79.

7. See the excellent and learned discussion of Ponce de León's literary inheritance in Olschki's essay, cited above.

8. *Ibid.*, pp. 363–65.

9. Irving B. Richman, *The Spanish Conquerors* (New Haven, Conn., 1919), pp. 73–74.

10. M. Oppenheim, *A History of the Administration of the Royal Navy and of Merchant Shipping in Relation to the Navy from 1509 to 1660* . . . (London, 1896), pp. 165–67; Douglas Bell, *Elizabethan Seamen* (London, 1936), pp. 90–97.

11. Alexander Ross (ed.), *The Marrow of History* (1650), p. 42.

12. A good account of the search for El Dorado prior to Raleigh's attempts may be found in V. T. Harlow's introduction to his edition of *The Discoverie of the large and bewtiful Empire of Guiana* (London: The Argonaut Press, 1928).

13. *Ibid.*, p. 17. Spelling, capitalization, and punctuation in quotations have been modernized.

14. *Ibid.*, pp. 56–57.

II

The Lure of Fish, Furs, Wine, and Silk

THE desire to get rich quickly is doubtless latent in most people, but it has been peculiarly characteristic of Americans since the first settler landed on these shores. The gold mania died hard, and English explorers for many years retained a persistent hope in the back of their heads that they would come upon gold or silver mines to equal the Spaniards' discoveries in Mexico and South America. The seamen who probed the long coastline of North America dreamed of gold mines that they might discover on the route to Cathay by way of the ever elusive Northwest Passage. Martin Frobisher, who made three voyages in search of this water route to China in the 1570's, wasted much of his time and energy mining worthless iron pyrites and loading his ships with this "fool's gold." On his first voyage in 1576 he brought back from the coast of Labrador a black rock showing bright flakes which he gave to Michael Lok, a London merchant, who was his financial backer. Although the best English metallurgists examined the stone and pronounced it worthless, Lok was not satisfied and at last found an Italian who told him what he wanted to hear: the stone was a piece of ore containing gold.

On Frobisher's second voyage, he took out a full complement of

Cornish miners, with tools and equipment. Finding large quantities of ore on the south coast of Baffin Land, all hands fell to mining and loading iron pyrites, a cargo that may have proved useful as ballast on the stormy voyage homeward, but it had no other value.

But charlatans continued to persuade the London merchants that the pyrites had a showing of gold, and these magnates backed a third and even more expensive expedition led by Frobisher to search for the Northwest Passage—and to mine more pyrites. Frobisher found neither gold nor the passage to Cathay, but his three voyages are illustrative of the persistence of the belief that both sources of easy wealth would be found. Even the Jamestown settlers—and many who came after them—still believed that the new world would in some fashion provide them with ready money and a competence to take home.

Englishmen were particularly eager to find sources of their own for commodities that they had been forced to obtain from Continental merchants, especially silk, dyes, drugs, and tropical products that came by way of Spain, Italy, or France. Nobody yet used the phrase "balance of payments," but English financiers were already worrying about the bullion that went out of the country for luxuries. If only Englishmen could find in the new world products that they imported from their enemies, the country's financial condition would be vastly improved, so the argument ran. If raw gold and silver could not be brought back, then the next best thing would be the commodities that English traders had to pay for in cash.

So much has been written about the exploits of the Elizabethan buccaneers that the popular imagination conceives of Elizabeth's daring seamen as principally concerned with thievery on the high seas. For many years, to be sure, every ship captain who sailed into the blue Atlantic from Plymouth or London hoped to intercept a Spanish treasure ship, but the early voyagers had other objectives as well. The English were already becoming a nation of shopkeepers, or at least a nation of traders and merchants.

One of the characteristics of the sixteenth century that distinguishes it from earlier periods is the new emphasis throughout western Europe upon trade. The Portuguese had early developed a bourgeois society bent upon exploiting trade with India and the East Indies. French traders from the Breton and Norman coasts also competed with the Portuguese, especially on the coast of Brazil. A little later the Dutch became the greatest trading nation in western Europe, with ships pushing, legally and illegally, into the distant ports of the world. The English were somewhat slower to realize the profits from seaborne trade, but from the second half of the sixteenth century onward, a few English sea captains were determined to share in the wealth from trade with the vast new lands across the seas.

Among the most daring of these early trader-seamen were the members of the Hawkins family of Plymouth. Richard Hakluyt tells of "old Mr. William Hawkins of Plymouth, a man for his wisdom, value, experience, and skill in sea causes much esteemed and beloved of King Henry VIII." [1] This William Hawkins was a pioneer who about 1530 showed other Englishmen the way to the Guinea coast and thence to Brazil. With "a tall and goodly ship of his own, of the burden of 250 tons, called the 'Paul of Plymouth' " he made three voyages to the coast of Africa, where he obtained Negro slaves, "elephants' teeth" (ivory), and some gold dust. Taking his slaves to Brazil, he sold them in a market already eager for Africans, who were much steadier laborers than the native Indians. From Brazil, Hawkins brought back dye woods (in great demand by the English cloth trade), sugar, and other exotic commodities. On his second voyage he also brought along an Indian "king," who caused some excitement in King Henry's court with his strange "apparel, behavior, and gestures." King Henry was astonished at his fellow sovereign's facial decorations: bones stuck in his cheeks and a precious stone "about the bigness of a pea" in his nether lip. Hakluyt reports that other English merchants followed Hawkins' trail during the next decade.

William's famous son, John, who was later knighted for his exploits against the Spaniards, was also a shrewd trader with the instincts of a merchant. A charming as well as a courageous man, he sailed to the Spanish Main and by his sheer audacity made friends there with the Spanish settlers, who saw no reason why they should not trade with the handsome stranger, especially since he brought African slaves from the coast of Guinea. Bartolomé de las Casas, the apostle to the Indians, in his zeal to abolish Indian slavery, had urged the substitution of African slavery, and the Spanish settlers had eagerly embraced the suggestion, for Indians in some areas were dying off and were often intractable. When Hawkins arrived in the West Indies in 1562 with slaves that he had obtained in Africa "partly by the sword and partly by other means" —the "other means" being purchase from native African slave traders—he was cordially welcomed and quickly disposed of his cargo.

On a second voyage in 1565 he obtained from the queen herself a great ship of 700 tons, the "Jesus of Lübeck." Hawkins had encountered another English ship, the "John the Baptist," also bound for the slave coast. No one thought it odd that these piously named ships should be engaged in the slave trade; indeed, few or none regarded trade in African slaves as iniquitous, and by the eighteenth century slave trading would become virtually an English monopoly that would bring great wealth to shareholders in the Royal African Company. John Hawkins was merely blazing a trail to Spanish America that through the centuries would prove infinitely profitable to his fellow-countrymen.

The account of Hawkins' second voyage, written by John Sparke, a gentleman aboard, who expressed his captain's views, showed that Hawkins and his colleagues were keenly alert to the commercial possibilities in the new lands that they observed. Hawkins, for example, was the first Englishman to realize that Florida had extraordinary potentials for wealth, not from gold, not from a fabulous spring of eternal youth, but from the lowly cattle industry—a development that had to wait until our time. But it is significant of Hawkins' shrewdness that he grasped this fact.

If many of Hawkins' immediate contemporaries were slow to

realize the possibilities for aggrandizement through trade in the commodities of the new world, it was not for lack of exhortation from a few propagandists, notably the two Richard Hakluyts. The younger Hakluyt's compilations of voyage literature and other writings were designed to arouse his countrymen to the opportunities awaiting them overseas. In a paper known by its abbreviated title of *A Discourse of Western Planting,* which Hakluyt prepared in 1584 for Queen Elizabeth at the behest of Sir Walter Raleigh, the preacher-propagandist presented a vast array of arguments to prove that England must seize a portion of the new world as a Christian and patriotic duty. While thus saving a critical portion of the world from the domination of Catholic Spain, England would obtain the sources of wealth then being monopolized by King Philip. Not only was Hakluyt prepared to base his arguments on high policy, but he was also ready with many practical suggestions for the attainment of colonial prosperity. He was not only in touch with expansionists like Raleigh and Sir Thomas Walsingham, he also had friends among the merchants of London, who understood what commodities were in greatest demand and what products were costing England an outlay of cash—cash that went to rivals, competitors, and traditional enemies.

Richard Hakluyt, the compiler of voyages, had an older cousin of the same name, a lawyer, who was even more concerned than the younger man in the economic benefits that would derive from the discovery of lands overseas. The lawyer Hakluyt was an associate and legal counsel for a group of merchants with contacts in Spain. He and his merchant friends were convinced that the drain of bullion from England in payment for essential products originating in or processed in Spain and Portugal might be stopped if England could find overseas possessions with a climate similar to that of the Iberian peninsula. The cloth industry of England required quantities of olive oil and large amounts of dyestuffs. The demand for wine from France and the Iberian countries was increasing. Hakluyt the lawyer in 1578 drew up a set of notes for the use of explorers, who were enjoined to seek territory that would produce tropical and semi-tropical commodities. These notes, later printed by the younger Hakluyt in *Divers Voyages* (1582), are an early expression of the mercantilist doctrine setting forth the relation of colonies to the mother country. As Hakluyt the lawyer and his merchant-clients believed, the new lands ought to provide raw materials and essential products of the land and at the same time consume cloth and other commodities of English manufacture.

These notes of the elder Hakluyt, printed under a heading stating that they were "framed by a gentleman heretofore to be given to one that prepared for a discovery and went not," described the kind of land and products that an English explorer ought to seek. Ideally, he should try to find an earthly paradise, a seat on the seaside with a river or bay behind where the colony's "own navy" could lie protected and come out to fight off hostile fleets. "This seat," Hakluyt continues, "is to be chosen in a temperate climate in sweet air, where you may possess always sweet water, wood, seacoals or turp, with fish, flesh, grain, fruits, herbs, and roots" necessary to the life of the settlers.

Hopefully, Hakluyt points out, the English may come upon some large territory of fertile soil. Having occupied this new land, they should

> so use the matter as we should not depend upon Spain for oils, sacks [sherry], raisins, oranges, lemons, Spanish skins, etc., nor upon France for wood, basalt, and Gascony wines, nor on Eastland for flax, pitch, tar, masts, etc. So we should not so exhaust our treasure and so exceedingly enrich our doubtful friends as we do, but should purchase the commodities that we want for half the treasure that now we do.

The foregoing notes by the elder Hakluyt on the desirability of finding a source for commodities that England had traditionally obtained from Mediterranean lands indicates the preoccupation of economic thinkers of the time with the loss of bullion in the purchase of olive oil, wine, and luxury products. Already the expansionists of the day were talking about colonies overseas, although success in that endeavor lay some years in the future. Men like Humphrey Gilbert, known to both the Hakluyts, were talking of means of circumventing the king of Spain and of freeing England from dependence upon Spanish products.

For centuries fishing had been a profitable undertaking for seamen from English ports. Long before Columbus, Bristol fishermen had frequented the waters between Ireland and Iceland. Very early in the sixteenth century English vessels, along with craft from Brittany and the Bay of Biscay, were making regular trips each summer to the fishing banks off Newfoundland. Their familiarity with these distant fishing grounds has led some patriotic Englishmen to believe that daring sailors from Bristol may have found their way to the American mainland before Columbus.[2] Be that as it may, English fishermen and merchants early recognized the desirability of laying claim to Newfoundland. Since they visited the island only in summer, they formed a favorable opinion of its climate and some even imagined that Newfoundland might produce dates, raisins, and figs. Indeed, for more than fifty years in the late sixteenth and early seventeenth centuries, expansionists continued to talk about the marvels of Newfoundland as if it were a tropical paradise. The more realistic among them, however, recognized Newfoundland's primary value as a base for profitable fisheries; its nearness to England also made it a convenient staging area for further advances upon the American mainland.

One of the early writers about the profits of fishing and the advantages of Newfoundland was a Kentish gentleman-adventurer, Anthony Parkhurst, who had been with Hawkins when he sailed up the Florida coast in 1565 and had later made voyages of his own to Newfoundland. Promoters in London, including Richard Hakluyt the elder, had apparently requested Parkhurst to make a survey of opportunities in Newfoundland and report. His first paper, written in the form of a letter dated 1577–78, perhaps to Edward Dyer, reveals a striking mercantilist concept of the profits obtainable from the fisheries.[3] Parkhurst begins by recalling to his correspondent's memory a meeting, "at my last being with you at the court," at which time he had observed "by your rejoicing heart what joy you conceived to hear anything that might benefit your country." The primary benefit that Parkhurst now has to discuss concerns "our trade of fishing, which might be made twice, yea, thrice as good as yet it is." Within the past five years, he points out, the fishing industry, centered upon Newfoundland, had expanded from "four sail of small barks to forty," half of the vessels being "worthy ships" able to bring home in one ship as much fish "as all the navy did before."

With this start, Parkhurst presents a reasoned argument for settling Newfoundland, opening a salt works, and establishing plants for processing fish. For all of its archaic phraseology, his letter sounds as modern as any report today on the establishment of new industries. The fishing industry requires vast supplies of salt, Parkhurst emphasizes, and the evaporation of salt in England is costly because of the scarcity of wood for fuel. In Newfoundland it could be evaporated easily near the place of greatest consumption, thus saving transporation of bulky supplies from England. Having been in Newfoundland and on the coast of North America in warm summer weather, Parkhurst thinks it possible to find "some apt place to make salt with the help of the sun, as in France and Spain" and suggests such a spot "about Cape Breton, being fenced from the cold air of the Isle by Cape Race" so that it is "very warm as at Rochelle."

With a permanent settlement and established works in Newfoundland, Parkhurst assures his correspondent that they could "keep people fishing half the year" and "make great store of dry fish." The expansion of the Newfoundland fishing industry would be infinitely preferable to "a Spanish voyage or other country's" because, in trade with Newfoundland, merchants would not have to carry away a great store of "ware nor money" but would enrich the commonwealth with fish processed by their own countrymen "sufficient to serve our realm and others from whence with it [the export of fish] we [could] bring home rich commodity." Thus Parkhurst, like the eighteenth-century mercantilists, conceived of a trade that would enable the home country to serve as a world distributor of products obtained from colonies which in turn would consume supplies manufactured in England.

An added benefit to the realm, Parkhurst stresses, would accrue from the growth of the navy and the increase of good mariners. Newfoundland would be an ideal training ground, the author indicates, because it offers no temptations to seafaring men away from home. Sailors perforce must remain honest and save their money, "for they find not in this country wine nor women." The common sailor's share in a Newfoundland voyage "is worth three times the wages they have for France, Spain, or Denmark," and since they cannot spend anything abroad, they bring their wages home, to the benefit of both their families and the commonwealth. "Thus can their wives, children, servants, and creditors witness with me the sweetness and profit of this voyage," Parkhurst adds piously.

Newfoundland not only can supply fish, but it offers an opportunity for iron mining and smelting, lumbering, and the raising of cattle and other livestock, Parkhurst asserts, and he stands ready in his next report to offer further proof of the country's habitability and utility to the commonwealth.

Parkhurst's letter deserves our attention because it is one of the earliest documents to emphasize the importance of developing the American fishing industry, a traffic that in time would become more important to Great Britain and her colonies than all the gold and silver that the British ever derived from the new world. About a year after his first report, Parkhurst wrote a letter to Richard Hakluyt the elder reiterating many of the things he had already said and giving further details of the number of fishermen frequenting Newfoundland waters for codfish and whales, the goodness of the country, and the economic benefits that would accrue to England if Newfoundland were settled as an English colony.[4] In this letter, dated from Bristol on November 13, 1578, Parkhurst also stressed the importance of the fur trade and of iron and copper deposits that he believed to exist on the mainland in Labrador. So eager was he for England to reap the profits of new enterprises in this part of the new world that he concluded his letter with the assertion that

> if you and your friend shall think me a man sufficient and of credit to seek the Isle of St. John or the River of Canada [the St. Lawrence], with any part of the firm land of Cape Breton, I shall give my diligence for the true and perfect discovery and leave some part of mine own business to further the same.

Fate did not decree that Parkhurst should lay claim to this portion of North America for the English. Another of his contemporaries and acquaintances, Sir Humphrey Gilbert, half brother of Sir Walter Raleigh, sailed into St. John's Harbor, Newfoundland, on August 5, 1583, bearing a commission from the queen to seize the land. Proclaiming the queen's law as now the law of Newfoundland, he read to the assembled fishermen his commission and affixed to a wooden pillar a leaden cast of the royal arms of England. Gilbert had added this misty island to the realm of England, and for the next half-century promoters continued to assert that here at last was a paradise that would produce most of the good things of the earth that the mother country needed.[5]

The hard-headed merchants of London and Bristol, who had as their spokesman Richard Hakluyt the lawyer, were convinced that the new world could supply commodities that they were accustomed to buy at great cost and risk from the Mediterranean countries, from the Baltic region, and from Russia. While his younger cousin emphasized the political and religious purposes of colonization, the elder Hakluyt labored unceasingly to drive home the notion of the rich economic possibilities overseas. When Raleigh was attempting to establish a colony on the coast of what is now North Carolina, Hakluyt drew up a remarkable document describing the economic objectives that such a colony should have and the means of attaining those ends. His paper, entitled "Inducements to the Liking of the Voyage Intended toward Virginia," was undoubtedly intended as a guide for leaders of the enterprise and probably circulated in manuscript among other promoters of colonization.[6]

At the beginning of his tract the elder Hakluyt comments that the enlargement of the queen's dominions would provide "an ample vent in time to come of the woolen clothes of England, especially those of the coarsest sort . . . and vent also of sundry [of] our commodities upon the tract of that firm land." Hakluyt would have been pleased if he could have foreseen the enormous demand that later developed among the Indians for English blankets. This type of trade was precisely what the early mercantilists dreamed of establishing. But Hakluyt was hopeful that the dominions about to be annexed to the queen's realm would also be a tropical or semi-tropical paradise that would supply wares now imported from alien lands: dyestuffs, oil, wine, hops, hemp, flax, salt, hides, furs, timber, naval stores, sugar, marble, and a variety of exotic foods, fruits, and other products.

The land that the colonists intended to settle, he points out, being in the latitude of Spain and Portugal, "may by our diligence yield unto us, besides wines and oils and sugars, oranges, lemons, figs, raisins, almonds, pomegranates, rice, raw silk such as come from Granada, and divers commodities for dyers, as anile and cochineal, and sundry other colors and materials." In payment for such products, Englishmen would ship in exchange articles of their own manufacture, "the labor of our poor people at home," items such as "hats, bonnets, knives, fishhooks, copper kettles, beads, looking glasses, bugles, and a thousand kind of wrought wares." Although the Indian trade was yet some distance in the future, Hakluyt described the classic pattern of barter that developed. He probably based his observations upon the experience of English traders on the coast of Guinea.

Hakluyt, like others who were promoting colonization, believed that the development of overseas trade would inevitably ensure the growth of the navy and the multiplication of skilled mariners. The flag would follow trade, in Hakluyt's reasoning, and the increase of sea power would parallel economic growth. "Receiving the same [imports from overseas] thence," he comments, "the navy, the human strength of this realm, our merchants and their goods, shall not be subject to arrest of ancient enemies and doubtful friends, as of late years they have been."

Another paper with a title similar to the foregoing document, drawn up by Hakluyt for the guidance of the expedition sent out by Raleigh in 1584, added certain other commodities that might be produced: whale oil, honey, feathers, casks and barrel staves, the "maintenance and increasing of silkworms for silk," and the "gathering of cotton, whereof there is great store." [7] The climate in the proposed area of occupation is so varied, he declares, that traders may return with their vessels laden with "all the commodities which we now receive from Barbary, Spain, Portugal, Italy, Dansk, Norway, and Muscovia better cheap than now we have them and not enrich our doubtful friends and infidels as now by our ordinary trade we do."

Master Hakluyt of the Middle Temple, having striven earnestly to teach the economic lessons that seemed so important to him if England were going to realize her potential greatness, must have been encouraged by a letter from Ralph Lane, dated from Raleigh's "new Fort in Virginia, this 3[rd of] September, 1585." [8] Lane assured him that the colonists had

> discovered the main [land] to be the goodliest soil under the cope of heaven, so abounding in sweet trees that bring such sundry rich and most pleasant gums, grapes of such greatness yet wild, as France, Spain, nor Italy hath no greater, so many sorts of apothecary drugs, such several kinds of flax, and one kind like silk, the same gathered of a grass as common there as grass is here. And now within these few days we have found here a Guinea wheat whose ear yieldeth corn for bread, 400 upon one ear, and the cane maketh very good and perfect sugar, also *Terra Samia,* otherwise *Terra sigillata.*

If Virginia only had cattle and horses, Lane thinks "no realm in Christendom" could compare with it. As it is, the colonists have found

that what commodities soever Spain, France, Italy, or the East
parts do yield unto us in wines of all sorts, in oils, in flax, in
rosins, pitch, frankincense, currants, sugars, and suchlike, these
parts do abound with the growth of them all, but being savages
that possess the land, they know no use of the same.

For the encouragement of the English clothiers, Lane adds this
comment: "The people naturally are most courteous and very de-
sirous to have clothes, but especially coarse cloth rather than silk;
coarse canvas they also like well of; but copper carrieth the price of
all, so it be made red." Unhappily, the inexperience of the colonists,
the ineptitude of the direction from home, and the war with Spain
prevented England from reaping the benefits of this rosy dream of
prosperity that Ralph Lane conjured up. Lane and his colonists
were to abandon the colony before a year was ended.

The propaganda carried on by the two Hakluyts and by many
other Elizabethan promoters was not wasted. The doctrines that
they preached about the economic as well as the political and stra-
tegic values in colonization overseas were not forgotten; and when
finally, under King James, permanent settlements were made in
North America, many of the economic goals stressed by the elder
Hakluyt were again emphasized.

Although the first years at Jamestown were disastrous because
many of the adventurers still dreamed of gold and easy wealth and
were not willing to undergo the labor required to establish the
colony on a sound basis, the settlers soon learned that they must
adapt to conditions as they were, not conditions that theorists had
wished to find. Armchair colonizers back in London were intent
upon making the Virginia colony a producer of exotic products
still imported from the Mediterranean countries. King James, the
royal pedant, from the depths of his knowledge set pen to paper
to tell the colonists how to produce silk and wine.

King James was determined to ensure a supply of silk and wine
from Virginia and to use his royal influence to magnify these
products instead of encouraging the cultivation of tobacco. He had

already expressed his repugnance to this weed in a tract entitled *A Counterblast to Tobacco* (1604). As a preface to a pamphlet by John Bonoeil, a Frenchman, explaining the breeding of silkworms, the making of raw silk, and the cultivation of grapes for wine, King James wrote a letter addressed to the Earl of Southampton, then treasurer of the Virginia Company. The king's epistle was used by the printer as the title to the whole treatise and it appeared in 1622 as *His Majesty's Gracious Letter to the Earl of Southampton . . . Commanding the Setting-Up of Silk Works and Planting of Vines in Virginia.* The king wrote as if he were making a royal proclamation:

Whereas we understand that the soil in Virginia naturally yieldeth store of excellent mulberry trees, we have taken into our princely consideration the great benefit that may grow to the adventurers and planters by the breed of silkworms and setting-up of silk works in those parts. And therefore of our gracious inclinations to a design of so much honor and advantage to the public, we have thought good, as at sundry other times, so now more particularly, to recommend it to your special care, hereby charging and requiring you to take speedy orders that our people there use all possible diligence in breeding silkworms and erecting silk works, that they rather bestow their travail in compassing this rich and solid commodity than in tobacco, which besides much unnecessary expense brings with it many disorders and inconveniences. And forasmuch as our servant, John Bonoeil, hath taken pains in setting down the true use of the silkworm, together with the art of silkmaking and of planting vines, and that his experience and abilities may much conduce to the advancement of this business, we do hereby likewise require you to cause his directions both for the said silk works and vineyards to be carefully put in practice throughout our plantations there, so the work may go on cheerfully and receive no more interruptions nor delays.[9]

Having in his royal wisdom settled the matter of silk and wine from Virginia, King James confidently expected the colonists to take his book of directions and immediately wax prosperous from the production of these two commodities. Like many other theorists who never stir from their libraries, the king believed that bookish directions would be enough to ensure success, especially if reinforced by a royal command.

Dutifully the Earl of Southampton in his capacity of treasurer of the Virginia Company appended his own letter to the treatise exhorting and commanding the colonists to bestir themselves in the making of silk and wine. He enjoined the governor and council to enforce the regulations requiring the planting of vines and mulberry trees and warned that no excuses would be tolerated. "Herein there can be no plea, either of difficulty or impossibility," he declared,

> but all the contrary appears by the natural abundance of these two excellent plants aforenamed everywhere in Virginia. Neither will such excuses be admitted, nor any other pretenses serve, whereby the business be at all delayed. And as we formerly sent at our great charge the French *vignerons* to you, to teach you their art, so for the same purpose we now commend this book unto you, to serve as an instructor to everyone, and send you store of them to be dispersed over the whole colony, to every master of a family one. Silk-feed you shall receive also by this ship, sufficient to store every man. So that there wants nothing but industry in the planter suddenly to bring the making of silk to its perfection, which either for their own benefit (we hope) they will willingly endeavor or by a wholesome and necessary severity they must be enforced.

No great imagination is required to visualize the scene in a Jamestown hut when the head of a family sat down with the king's book of directions and contemplated it and the governor's command to make silk and wine. Even if the settler were literate enough to read the book with comprehension, the practical difficulties that he faced with all the other labor that he had to perform made silk production and the care of vineyards mere fantasies of dreamers back in London. The skill and the labor required for the production of silk were so great that silk making never became a profitable enterprise in the English colonies, although the delusion persisted for two centuries. Nor did the climate of Virginia and the other colonies prove benign to the planters of vineyards. Wine making also remained a delusion that persisted for generations. Another influence, equally effective in curbing the development of exotic industries, was the relative ease with which tobacco could be grown and the great profits from its sale. King James might rail against its use, but even he soon learned that revenue from Virginia tobacco was important to his own exchequer and essential to the life of the colony.

While the theorizers in London continued to look to Virginia and elsewhere on the North American mainland for sources of exotic commodities, a few realists were expressing the belief that riches could be had from humbler products. One of the emphatic propagandists for a more realistic appraisal of the opportunities for wealth in America was Captain John Smith. His hard-headed good sense had helped save the Virginia colony in its early days, and he retained his interest in colonial enterprise. During the spring and summer of 1614, in command of two ships, he returned to the North American coast, exploring the shoreline from Maine southward. While his crews fished for cod and dried their catch on shore, Smith in a small boat probed the coast and traded with the Indians for furs. He returned to England with a profitable cargo of fish and furs and with notes for a book that he presently published as *The Description of New England* (1616), a tract that stirred the interest of English merchants and traders in the potential profits from codfish, beaver, marten, and other skins obtainable in New England.

Smith of course was not the first to realize that both fish and furs were to be found in great abundance in this region. How

early Englishmen began to catch fish on the New England coast
and trade with the Indians, no one knows, for these seamen and
traders were notoriously close-mouthed about the sources of their
cargoes. But by the early years of the seventeenth century, voyages
to New England were becoming fairly frequent. Bartholomew
Gosnold, who made a trading voyage along the coast in 1602, was
so impressed with the multitude of fish that he named one point
of land Cape Cod. In 1603 Martin Pring, another adventurous
trader, discovered Plymouth harbor and came home to tell about
the opportunities in the region. In 1605 George Weymouth made
a profitable voyage of trade and exploration and impressed his
backers with the profits from the fur trade. He also brought home
five kidnapped Indians who created a great wonder in London. A
settlement on the Kennebec River in Maine in the late summer of
1607, led by George Popham and Raleigh Gilbert, was a failure,
but the disgruntled colonists returned home with a valuable cargo
of furs and stories of profits that could be made by fishing and
trading with the Indians. Because of these earlier expeditions, the
country was receptive to Smith's enthusiastic tract on New England
when he published it in 1616.

Smith, who himself had looked for gold and silver mines, set
out to convince his countrymen that greater wealth could be seined
from the sea than could be dug from the earth—at least the parts
of the earth that he had visited. He expressed the wish that he
could settle a colony in New England, where he would rather live
than in any other of the four parts of the world. And the main
staple for profit in that delectable region, he insisted, would be
fish. Though fish "may seem a mean and base commodity," he
asserted, the fishing industry might be of immense profit to England. To prove his point he cited the instance of the Dutch who
"by fishing at a great charge and labor in all weathers in the open
sea are made a people so hardy and industrious." The Dutch trade
their fish to the Baltic people for other mean commodities—wood,
flax, pitch, tar, rosin, and cordage—which they then sell to the
French, Spaniards, Portuguese, and English, and thus grow richer

and stronger than Venice or countries twice their size. All of this prosperity and power the Dutch have obtained from "this contemptible trade of fish." Fishing, says Smith,

> is their mine and the sea the source of those silvered streams of all their virtue, which hath made them now the very miracle of industry, the pattern of perfection for these affairs, and the benefit of fishing is that *primum mobile* that turns all their spheres to this height of plenty, strength, honor, and admiration.

By exploiting the fishing opportunities of New England, Smith maintained, Englishmen might do as well as the industrious Hollanders. The fish in New England are fatter and more numerous than those off Newfoundland, he pointed out, and the season is much longer.

Smith's treatise not only described the varieties of fish to be had on the New England coast but it also gave practical advice about methods of fishing, preparing the fish, and the best seasons for catching the many kinds of fish abundant in New England waters.

But fish were not the only resources of New England that Smith emphasized. From his own experience he knew that the fur trade held a promise of rich profits. He mentioned the quantities of muskrat, beaver, marten, otter, and black fox that the French yearly took out of the northern region and added wistfully, "25,000 [skins] this year were brought from those northern parts into France, of which trade we may have as good part as the French if we take good courses." In addition to fish and furs, Smith also stressed the value of wood products that the forests of New England could provide. Here was a realist, a trader who had personal knowledge of the regions of the North Atlantic seaboard, who foresaw the lines of economic development that would make both England and her colonies prosperous. He exerted all the influence that he could muster to divert promoters from the exotic to the humbler sources of wealth. Unlike the theorists at court, Smith had seen with his own eyes the products of North America that promised a rich trade, and he was prepared to advocate those forms of enterprise that promised the most practical results, even if his advice went against the cherished dreams of his sovereign.

The promoters of the generation before Smith—men like Richard Hakluyt the elder—were eager to free themselves from economic dependence upon Spain, Portugal, and France. They saw their opportunity in the new world, and their planning was based upon their needs rather than upon the known potentials of the country overseas. This insistence upon planning in accordance with the needs of the homeland, sometimes in obvious disregard of the potentials of the colonies, persisted for generations and led to much wasted effort and sometimes to disaster. This attitude, often as unrealistic as King James's belief that his book of directions would result in profitable silk production, was the cause of infinite friction between the colonials and the men who sat in snug offices in London. As the mercantilist doctrine became an established dogma in the later seventeenth and early eighteenth centuries, the Lords of Trade continued to echo suggestions that appear as early as Richard Hakluyt the elder. In the light of experience, many of these suggestions proved viable and useful; but others, for one reason or another, could not be carried to fruition, however desirable they may have been for either colonists or mother country. Some of the delusions, as well as the successes, had important implications for later colonial development.

Notes

1. Clements R. Markham (ed.), *The Hawkins' Voyages*. Hakluyt Society (London, 1878), No. 57, p. 3. A good account of the Hawkins' exploits is James A. Williamson, *Hawkins of Plymouth* (London, 1949).

2. See David B. Quinn, "The Argument for the English Discovery of America between 1480 and 1494," *Geographical Journal*, CXXVII (1961), 277–85.

3. The interest in fisheries and the mercantilist attitude of these early promoters are discussed by Miss E. G. R. Taylor, *The Original Writings and Correspondence of the Two Richard Hakluyts*. Hakluyt Society, Series 2, LXXVI (London, 1935), pp. 14 ff. Miss Taylor reprints Parkhurst's letter, pp. 123–27.

4. Taylor, *Original Writings,* pp. 127–34.

5. See Richard Eburne, *A Plain Pathway to Plantations,* edited by Louis B. Wright (Ithaca, N.Y., 1962), Introduction, and Louis B. Wright, *Religion and Empire* (Chapel Hill, N.C., 1943), *passim.*

6. It is reprinted by Miss Taylor, *Original Writings,* pp. 327–38, from John Brereton's *Discovery of the North Part of Virginia* (1602). Brereton appears to have altered the original title to fit his own destination in the north, for the text refers to a region in the latitude of 36, 37, and 40 degrees, whereas the title as Brereton printed it reads: "Inducements to the Liking of the Voyage intended toward Virginia in 40 and 42 degrees of latitude, written 1585 [more likely 1584], by M. Richard Hakluyt the elder, sometime student of the Middle Temple."

7. Taylor, *Original Writings,* pp. 339–43. The document is printed from Sloane MS 1447.

8. *Ibid.,* pp. 346–47. Miss Taylor reprints Lane's letter from Hakluyt's *Principal Navigations* (1589).

9. First printed in 1622 (*Short Title Catalogue,* 14,378), the king's and Southampton's letters were reprinted by Samuel Purchas, *Purchas His Pilgrims* (1625). They appear in the Maclehose edition (Glasgow, 1906), XIX, 154–57.

III

Cures for All the Ills of Mankind

THE spices that Europe had long imported from the East and that were such an important part of the caravan trade in the late Middle Ages were not merely required to improve the flavor of food—as necessary as that was in the days before refrigeration. Spices were essential to the pharmacopoeia of the day, and along with the spices came additional products used in the compounding of drugs. These products ranged from gums and herbs to such strange items as mummy, bezoar stones, and unicorn horns. The demand for drugs was probably greater than that for spices used in the preparation of food, if we except pepper, which was always eagerly sought. With the opening up of the new world, the commerce in drugs and the raw materials for drugs received a whole new dimension, for Europe came to believe that cures for all the ailments that beset mankind might be found across the seas. Ponce de León might look for a fountain of youth, but more practical adventurers were glad to bring back bales and barrels of weeds, bark, roots, and rocks that were readily bought by the apothecaries. Not only did the new world promise prosperity but its products also held out the hope of good health.

The Spanish were aware of the possibilities of finding health-giving drugs, and as early as 1525 Oviedo y Valdez, the Viceroy of Mexico, reported on the medical products of the new world. The most influential work, however, was a publication by another Spaniard, Nicolás Monardes, a prosperous physician of Seville, who brought out in 1569 *Dos libros, el uno que trata de todas las cosas que traen de nuestras Indias Occidentales, que sirven al uso de la Medicina, y el otro que trata de la Piedra Bezaar, y de Yerva Escuerçonera.* Monardes in 1571 published a third part of his treatise describing still other medicinal products, and finally in 1574 he brought all three parts together in a definitive edition of a work that soon was known throughout Europe.

An English merchant who had long been engaged in the Spanish trade, John Frampton, translated Monardes' treatise of 1574 and published it in 1577 with a promising title: *Joyful News out of the New Found World: Wherein Is Declared the Rare and Singular Virtues of Diverse and Sundry Herbs, Trees, Oils, Plants, and Stones, with Their Applications, As Well for Physic as Chirurgery; the Said, Being Well Applied, Bringeth Such Present Remedy for All Diseases As May Seem Altogether Incredible, Notwithstanding by Practice Found out to Be True. Also the Portraiture of the Said Herbs Very Aptly Described. Englished by John Frampton, Merchant.* The translator dedicated his work to Sir Edward Dyer, an associate of Richard Hakluyt the elder in promoting economic opportunities overseas.

Frampton observes in his dedication that the commodities described by Monardes have already become articles of commerce and are being imported from Spain into England. These American drugs, he indicates, have superseded many older remedies.

And since the aforesaid medicines mentioned in the same work of Dr. Monardes are now by merchants and others brought out of the West Indies into Spain and from Spain hither into England by such as doth daily traffic thither, and that the excellency of these herbs, trees, oils, plants, stones, etc., hath been known to be so precious a remedy for all manner of diseases and hurts that may hap unto man, woman, or child, they have fled very much from the old order and manner of physic which was used before that this was known, as things not so healthful as these are, and by great experience thereof in Spain and other countries thoroughly and effectuously proved to do the effects which is contained in this book.

Since Dyer was known to be a man concerned with the good of the commonwealth, Frampton was pleased to launch his book of American remedies under his protection.[1] The treatise was immediately popular and three editions had appeared by 1596. It evidently created a sensation among doctors, apothecaries, and laymen, who were ready to believe any wondrous thing about the new world.

So great was the excitement over American drugs that Timothy Bright, moved with nationalistic zeal, published *A Treatise Wherein Is Declared the Sufficiency of English Medicines for [the] Cure of All Diseases Cured with Medicine* (1580). A new edition of Bright's tract in 1615 noted on the title page a supplement "Whereunto is added a collection of medicines growing for the most part within our English climate."

The notion that a remedy could be discovered wherever a disease was found had been elaborated by Paracelsus and others as the doctrine of signatures, but readers of Frampton's book were ready to believe that the Almighty had been keeping a reserve stock of medicines in the new world against the time when Europeans would need them most. Since English doctors had been unable to find cures for all indigenous diseases within the British Isles, perhaps the search would be easier in the new world, where all good things were reported to exist. At any rate, the hope of discovering miraculous remedies overseas became a persistent dream that has not yet vanished from the purlieus of folk medicine.

For the Elizabethan, the professional basis for the search began with Frampton's translation of Monardes' book, and for that reason some attention to its contents will be useful for an understanding of the commerce that developed in American drugs and products believed to have curative values.

Not only was the new world believed to be the source of universal cures but unfortunately it was also believed to be the source of a dread disease. Columbus' sailors were said to have brought back a plague, hitherto unknown, that quickly became endemic throughout Europe. The plague was syphilis. Modern investigation has shown that syphilis probably existed in both Europe and Asia from early times, and that from the twelfth century onward inunctions of mercury had been used as a remedy for the malady.[2] Various nations of Europe attributed it to their neighbors: thus, in France it was known as the Neapolitan sickness; but in Naples it was the French pox. Everyone shifted responsibility for the disease to another, and it was easy to blame the heathen of America. For reasons that medical men find obscure, a flare-up in virulence occurred in the first half of the sixteenth century and the doctors of all Europe started looking desperately for new remedies. If the ailment was of new world origin, then, according to the doctrine of the day, the new world ought to provide a cure.

Although syphilis may have had an ancient origin in Asia, the medical profession in Europe in the sixteenth century eagerly embraced the notion that the outbreak coinciding with the early voyages of discovery resulted from infection brought back by sailors. In 1539 Dr. Diaz de Isla published his *Tractado contra el mal serpentino,* in which he described the disease as having been brought from Santo Domingo by Columbus' sailors, who spread the infection in Barcelona in April, 1493. Others had already mentioned the West Indian origin of the disease, but Diaz de Isla gives the most circumstantial account. He was followed a little later by Monardes, who also described the ailment as having originated in Santo Domingo. He related that Columbus stopped at Naples in 1493 on his return from the West Indies with a number of Indian men and women. These Indians, Monardes insisted, communicated the disease to both French and Spanish soldiers, from whom it spread abroad. At any rate, the popularity of Monardes' book gave wide currency to this story.

Since Monardes was convinced of the American origin of the malady, he prescribed several American remedies, which were soon in great demand. Perhaps the most famous of the curative drugs was derived from a tree indigenous to Santo Domingo called in Frampton's translation of Monardes "guaiacan." This is guaiacum, or *lignum vitae,* a tree of the caltrop family. In the presence of various oxidizing agents, resin from guaiacum has the property of changing color. This characteristic was soon observed and helped to recommend guaiacum to doctors and apothecaries, who could thus give an ocular demonstration to their patients of its powerful qualities.

Monardes has minute directions for boiling the wood and bark of the guaiacum "in a new pot" and finally storing the liquor in a glass vessel until the physician is ready to dose his patient, who must start the day with ten ounces of the infusion hot enough to make him "sweat well." At four-hour intervals throughout the day the patient must drink the hot guaiacum infusion, sweat, and then eat raisins, almonds, and biscuit. No other drink or diet must be taken for fifteen days unless the patient shows notable weakness, in which case he may add a bit of chicken to his diet. After one or more series of such treatments the patient might hope to be cured of "many infirmities incurable, where other medicines could not do this effect," says Monardes.

Guaiacum became a part of the European pharmacopoeia and was regarded as a remedy for sundry other ailments besides syphilis. Guaiacum resin remained in the pharmacopoeia until recent times as a constituent of popular remedies for gout, rheumatism, and skin diseases. In the commerce of the sixteenth and seventeenth centuries, guaiacum, or *lignum vitae,* was a popular commodity.

Among other American plants commended by Monardes for use in the treatment of venereal diseases were China smilax, sarsaparilla, and sassafras. All of these became important articles of commerce, and all retained their popularity for centuries, not only as specifics for venereal diseases but for many other ailments. Sarsaparilla and sassafras are still being marketed in certain areas of this country for use in folk remedies. Each spring in Washington, D.C., one can buy in some of the chain grocery stores small bundles of sassafras chips and roots, neatly packaged in cellophane bags. They are bought by customers who boil them into an aromatic tea, believed to be good for spring fever and for "purifying the blood."

Monardes recommended infusions of the China smilax for all sorts of skin diseases, as well as for gout, rheums, sciatica, pestilent agues, dropsy, liver complaints, and bad complexions. Sarsaparilla, he thought, was only a little behind the China smilax in virtue. He himself had concocted a syrup of sarsaparilla useful for most of the ailments that the China smilax cured—and pleasanter to take. Infusions of sarsaparilla, good for women's diseases and for "cold humors," says Monardes, "doth marvelously dissolve winds." In addition, a course of treatment consisting of constant drinking of sarsaparilla will cure old and evil humors and diseases which the patients never thought to be healed of.

Sassafras, a tree that Monardes described as growing in Florida, provided wood and roots "of great virtues and great excellencies" useful in healing "grievous and variable diseases." The sweet smell of sassafras had led the early explorers of Florida to think that they had come upon cinnamon trees, but they quickly came to believe that this new aromatic tree had virtues greater than those of the cinnamon—and probably equally profitable in commerce. Scarcely a disease that one can think of will resist sassafras tea, if we can believe the good doctor of Seville, who vows that he has had experience in the use of this wonderful panacea. Digestive troubles, kidney ailments, chills and fever, headaches, colds, toothache, bad breath, and even infertility all respond to sassafras water. No advertiser of vitamins could go further in praising his pills than Dr. Monardes went in recommending sassafras as a restorative of the appetite. So potent was its effect that soldiers on short rations had to avoid taking sassafras tea lest it stir their hunger beyond any capacity to find food to satisfy their ravening appetites.

The news of the virtues of sassafras quickly spread through Europe and excited physicians, apothecaries, and merchants. When the first settlers landed at Jamestown in 1607, they began eagerly to search for sassafras, which, to their joy, they discovered growing in abundance on the peninsula between the James and York rivers. Captain Newport loaded his vessels with the wood and roots of sassafras.

In the first letter sent back by the Council of the colony in Virginia to the Virginia Company of London, a letter that Captain Newport took with him on his return, the local authorities at Jamestown complained of the way the sailors had greedily dug up all the sassafras in reach:

> Our easiest and richest commodity, being sassafras roots, were gathered up by the sailors with loss and spoil of many of our tools and with drawing of our men from our labor. We wish that they may be dealt with so that all the loss neither fall on us nor them. I believe they have thereof two tons at least, which if they scatter abroad at their pleasure will pull down our price for a long time; we leave this to your wisdoms.[3]

During the early years of settlement, the Jamestown colony found that sassafras was one of the most profitable commodities, but, as the Council feared, they soon glutted the London market and brought down the price. Nevertheless, though from time to time an oversupply spoiled the market, sassafras remained for many years a steady export from Virginia. In 1610 the Virginia Company of London listed among products particularly desired in London both sassafras and sarsaparilla. Englishmen in the early seventeenth century were avidly drinking sassafras tea and hopefully believing that their bodily afflictions would magically disappear. At least they had the authority of learned doctors for holding to these beliefs, and such is the power of faith that doubtless sassafras did work many cures.

Not all of the remedies that Dr. Monardes promised from the new world were vegetable; some were animal and mineral, and of these the most famous was the bezoar stone: calcium phosphate concretions, taken from the alimentary canals of ruminant animals and other beasts.

In the Orient, bezoar stones, principally from goats and gazelles, had long been prized as antidotes to poison. The Spaniards had discovered that Peruvian llamas were a source of bezoar stones, which they soon advertised as possessing vast medicinal virtues, particularly against poisoned arrows and tainted meat. Calcareous secretions from other animals also found great favor among the medical explorers. Stones from the stomachs of alligators and crocodiles, applied to the forehead and temples, were good for chills and fever. The bony tail of the armadillo, an animal that the explorers had never before seen, also proved medically useful. The powdered bone, made into small balls and inserted in the ears, was a specific against earache, deafness, and ringing in the head.

Among the great number of products of the new world that Dr. Monardes believed of medicinal value, few received higher praise or had greater significance for the English than tobacco. The second part of Monardes' work, published in 1571, begins, in Frampton's translation, with a section headed "Of the Tobacco and of His Great Virtues."

Columbus' sailors on the first voyage observed that the Indians in Cuba carried burning sticks to light leaf-wrapped herbs which they smoked—the first Havana cigars noticed by Europeans. The early explorers found that the smoking of tobacco was widespread among the Indians, and Europeans were quick to adopt the habit. Tobacco plants were first introduced into Spain as ornamental garden plants, according to Monardes; but, having discovered the "marvelous medicinal virtues" of the herb, Spaniards now "do use it more for his virtues than for his fairness."

The enumeration of the healing qualities of tobacco requires more than twenty pages in the modern reprint of Frampton's translation. Monardes points out that only the leaves of the plants have healing qualities but that experiments may prove that the roots are also useful. The leaves, being powdered, will glue together and heal fresh wounds, cure old sores, and bring an injured man to perfect health. But this is only one of the many virtues of tobacco. A poultice of tobacco leaves, put hot upon the head, will cure all "cold causes" and rheums. A syrup of tobacco is good for congestions in the chest, and the smoke of the leaves, "being taken at the mouth," is good for congestions and for shortness of breath. Hot dried leaves of tobacco, mixed with a few warm ashes and placed on the stomach, will relieve sundry griefs in that portion of the body. Indeed, hot applications of dried tobacco or hot poultices of the green leaves will relieve almost any congestion, pains in the joints, swellings, and chilblains. A little ball of tobacco chewed and applied to an aching tooth is a sovereign remedy. Tobacco, both chewed and smoked in a little cane, has the virtue of relieving weariness and refreshing the spirit, as the Indians have often demonstrated on long journeys.

Monardes adds an account of the experiments of his friend "Master John Nicot," counselor to the king of France and ambassador from France to Portugal in 1559–61. When Nicot was visiting a Portuguese prison, the keeper gave him some tobacco plants, lately brought from Florida. Other accounts say that a Flemish merchant gave him the plants. Whatever the source, Nicot cultivated the herb and began to test the use of the leaves medicinally. His cook, having nearly cut off his thumb with a chopping knife, applied to Nicot for help. Promptly the ambassador slapped a tobacco poultice on the damaged thumb, which presently was completely healed. The fame of the herb and of Nicot's use of it spread to France, where tobacco became a remedy prescribed for almost every ailment. Jean Nicot gave his name to the botanical designation of the tobacco plant—and thus gained immortality.

The popularity of Monardes' book throughout Europe, and the interest that Frampton's translation aroused in England, stirred both physicians and merchants to seek the drugs and medicinal products that he described. His enthusiastic commendation of tobacco gave the herb a prestige that it might not otherwise have acquired so rapidly.

Precisely when tobacco was first known in England is a controversial question, but probably John Hawkins brought back tobacco and pipes from one of his voyages.[4] Edmund Howes, who published a continuation of John Stow's *Annals or General Chronicle of England* in 1615, declares that "Tobacco was first brought and made known in England by Sir John Hawkins about the year one thousand, five hundred sixty-five, but not used by Englishmen in many years after, though at this day [1615], commonly used by most men and many women." [5] A note by Howes says, "Sir Walter Raleigh brought first the knowledge of tobacco." In popular legend, Raleigh is credited with the introduction of smoking, and, as we can see, this attribution begins very early. Certainly Raleigh was known as an inveterate smoker himself, and his example undoubtedly popularized a habit rapidly taken up by the courtiers and those who aped them.

Others besides Monardes gave tobacco a good name and commended its health-inducing qualities. Charles Estienne and Jean Liebault in 1567 published in Paris *L'Agriculture et maison rustique,* a work widely read in Europe and translated into English in 1600, which praised the medicinal virtues of the plant. In 1571 a Flemish botanist, Matthias de L'Obel, published in England an herbal dedicated to Queen Elizabeth, *Stirpium adversaria nova,* which asserted that tobacco was already being grown in Portugal, France, Belgium, and England, and the author did not know which country had received the greatest benefit from it. He might also have mentioned Spain as another country where tobacco was already naturalized. Tobacco, L'Obel asserted, "should be preferred to any panacea, even the most celebrated," because of its beneficial effects on external and internal ailments.[6]

Englishmen took up the paean of praise of tobacco's healing qualities and continued to magnify the importance of the herb. In 1595 Anthony Chute published *Tobacco: The Distinct and Several Opinions of the Late and Best Physicians That Have Written of the Divers Natures and Qualities Thereof,* a book generally called the first original work by an Englishman on the subject. Chute approves of smoking, but only for medicinal reasons, and he recommends that the patient confine himself to a pipe before breakfast.[7] English herbals and other works added their recommendations of tobacco. Dr. Raphael Thorius about 1610 even wrote a poem on tobacco in Latin hexameters, *Hymnus tabaci,* which circulated in manuscript until it was finally printed in 1625. During the plague years of the early seventeenth century, English writers recommended tobacco as a preservative against the pestilence, and it was long believed, even down to modern times, that tobacco smoke would help to ward off infection.

When the plague was raging in London in 1665, William Kemp published *A Brief Treatise of the Nature, Causes, Signs, Preservation from, and Cure of the Pestilence* in which he recommended pipe smoking as a preservative of health in time of infection. His directions provided an aromatic touch that may seem a bit too exotic for modern tastes, for he suggested adding a bit of nutmeg to one's pipe tobacco. Kemp's praise of tobacco was unbounded. Tobacco smoking, he says, is a defense against bad air and disperses "venomous vapors." It is good for all ages and sexes, "young and old, men and women, the sanguine, the choleric, the melancholy, the phlegmatic [who] take it without any manifest inconvenience." Pipe smoking is beneficial under any circumstances, for "it quencheth thirst and yet will make one more able and fit to drink." It also will relieve hunger without destroying the appetite and "is agreeable with mirth and sadness, with feasting and with fasting; it will make one rest that wants sleep and will make one waking that is drowsy." [8] In short, tobacco smoke is both a preservative and a comfort that mankind should treasure.

So great was the prestige of tobacco as a prophylactic against plague that during the epidemic of 1665 schoolboys at Eton were whipped for not smoking, if we can believe a report of Thomas Hearne, the antiquary. Other schoolboys carried in the satchels with their books pipes filled with tobacco, and, at an appointed time in the morning, they stopped for a smoke under the direction of a master who instructed them in the proper way to hold their pipes and inhale.[9]

In the same plague year that Kemp was recommending pipe smoking, Dr. Gideon Harvey, in *A Disourse of the Plague,* made a revealing statement about the economics of medical practice in his day by dividing remedies into two classifications: one list gave "Preservations for the Rich" and another "Preservations for the Poor." As Miss Sarah Augusta Dickson points out in her excellent book, *Panacea or Precious Bane,* the price of tobacco had gone down to a point where even London's poor could afford it. "In 1603 when a severe epidemic of the plague raged in England," Miss Dickson asserts, "a pound of tobacco, then obtained only from the Spanish colonies, sold in England for 33 shillings. In 1625, another plague year, Virginia tobacco fetched three shillings a pound. In 1665 the poor could afford to buy the prophylactic at the price of eight pence a pound." [10] The price was to continue to decline, one might add, much to the distress of the growers on Chesapeake Bay.

The almost universal acclaim of tobacco as a plant of curative powers beyond the dreams of physicians—a wonder drug that held out hope to untold numbers of the afflicted—did not go completely unchallenged. The medical profession always has its questioners who, fortunately for the human race, maintain a wise skepticism about panaceas that in every generation capture the public imagination—and arouse wistful hope. Although the great proportion of professional opinion in the sixteenth and seventeenth centuries commended the use of tobacco for medicinal purposes, and did not disapprove of its use for pleasure, a few physicians and others from time to time wrote against it. For example, in 1602 a physician who signed himself I. H. published *Work for Chimney Sweeps, or A Warning for Tobacconists* [Smokers] in which he printed a warning on the title page: "Better be choked with English hemp/Than poisoned with Indian tobacco." In the preface he admits that many learned physicians, including Monardes, had commended the use of tobacco, but that he feels fully competent to dissent, "having . . .

solid reasons and true experience on my side to countervail their authorities founded rather on opinion than on certain science or demonstrations."

The most famous attack on the use of tobacco came not from a physician but from no less a person than King James himself. Summoning all of his royal authority, the English Solomon, as he liked to be called, delivered himself in 1604 of *A Counterblast to Tobacco,* a tract that vehemently condemned tobacco as an evil straight from hell, useless as a drug and harmful to the morals and manners of the realm. King James warned that physicians had opened the bodies of victims of the tobacco habit and had found them as sooty inside as kitchen flues. A few years earlier, a German traveler in London, Thomas Platter, had also reported that "someone told me that after the death of one man [a great smoker] it was found that his veins were covered inside with a coating of soot." [11] King James declared that his subjects had become slaves of tobacco and were guilty of

> sinning against God, harming yourselves both in persons and goods, and . . . making yourselves to be wondered at by all foreign civil nations, and, by all strangers that come among you, to be scorned and contemned: a custom loathsome to the eye, hateful to the nose, harmful to the brain, dangerous to the lungs, and in the black stinking fume thereof nearest the horrible Stygian smoke of the pit that is bottomless.

No opponent of cigarette smoking today could go beyond King James in his condemnation of the use of tobacco.

But the King had undertaken the labor of Sisyphus. Despite his opposition—and despite the occasional physician who found tobacco evil—the use of the herb was already so firmly established in England that nothing could stop it. Before King James had ascended the throne in 1603, smoking had become a fashionable practice. Queen Elizabeth herself is supposed to have indulged in an occasional pipe, and her courtiers and maids of honor certainly were addicted to tobacco. The literature of the late sixteenth and early seventeenth centuries is full of allusions to pipe smoking. Some writers satirize the vanities of gallants who waste their time and substance in this newfangled habit, but they all testify to the widespread use of tobacco for pleasure. Taught by physicians that tobacco had curative powers and then lulled into its use by the soothing comforts of smoking, Englishmen were not likely to curtail the use of the Indian weed. Indeed, from the late sixteenth century onward the consumption of tobacco steadily increased, to the benefit of the finances of Great Britain, if not to the improvement of its health, as the early advocates had promised.

The promoters of English colonies were hoping for some commodity that would ensure the financial salvation of their enterprise. The early cargoes of sassafras carried with them the hopes of the promoters for just such a commodity, but sassafras, unfortunately for them, was not habit-forming, and Englishmen could drink just so much sassafras tea for the good of their healths. The colonizers were not yet aware that the source of infinite wealth was symbolized by the smoke curling from the pipes of the Indians whom they found on the coasts of North Carolina and Virginia.

Thomas Harriot, the scientist who accompanied Raleigh's colony to Roanoke Island in 1585, wrote three paragraphs on tobacco in *A Brief and True Report of the New Found Land of Virginia* (1588), but these paragraphs were fraught with tremendous implications for the future. Of the Indians' use of tobacco, Harriot reports:

> The leaves thereof being dried and brought into powder, they use to take the fume or smoke thereof by sucking it through pipes made of clay into their stomach and head, from whence it purgeth superfluous phlegm and other gross humors . . . whereby their bodies are notably preserved in health and know not many grievous diseases wherewithal we in England are oftentimes afflicted.

These first colonists, after a year's trial, gave up and went home in a fleet commanded by Francis Drake, but they carried with them the incipient habit of smoking and the belief that tobacco was a commodity of medicinal virtue if not of commercial value. Harriot comments:

> We ourselves during the time we were there used to suck it after their [the Indians'] manner, as also since our return, and have found many rare and wonderful experiments of the virtues thereof, of which the relation would require a volume by itself. The use of it by so many of late, men and women of great calling as else, and some learned physicians also, is sufficient witness.

When the English in 1607 finally made a settlement at Jamestown that endured, they observed that the Indians of that region smoked tobacco and prized the weed as a holy herb bestowed upon them by their gods. But Virginia tobacco was sharp and biting to the tongue and held little promise in commerce. The native tobacco was a species now called *Nicotiana rustica*. It did not appeal to English or most west European tastes, but, oddly enough, it later found favor in Bulgaria and other parts of eastern Europe, where it is still cultivated. John Rolfe, famous for his marriage to Pocahontas, was the first to experiment with a variety of tobacco, *Nicotiana tabacum*, that the Spaniards and Portuguese were already cultivating and popularizing. Drake, apparently, in 1585 had taken back to England specimens and seeds of this variety, which he had acquired on the coast of South or Central America. From some source Rolfe obtained seeds of *Nicotiana tabacum* and in 1612-13 produced in Virginia the first crop of salable tobacco. Though he did not realize it at the time, he had assured Virginia of prosperity and riches for centuries to come. More than that, he had also assured the English government of a permanent source of revenue and the English merchants of a commodity that would guarantee them prosperity.

In March, 1614, Rolfe shipped four barrels of tobacco to London in the ship "Elizabeth." This was the beginning of the great tobacco trade that enriched both England and the colonies in the later seventeenth and eighteenth centuries.[12] Within two years, the little colonies of Virginia and Bermuda were beginning to grow tobacco on a commercial scale. By 1617 they shipped to England 18,839 pounds of tobacco, which they increased by the next year to 49,528 pounds. The price of tobacco in the colony was fixed by the Virginia Assembly in 1619 at three shillings a pound, but it remained at that price for only a few seasons. If we estimate the purchasing power of money at ten times its present value—and it was probably greater than this—we can see what a boon tobacco growing was to colonists who had previously been grubbing up sassafras roots, hewing out clapboards, and looking for sarsaparilla in order to find commodities salable in London.

The settlers at Jamestown, with hysterical eagerness, set about growing tobacco to the neglect of all other activities. They planted the streets and waste places around the town in tobacco and refused to plant corn needed for their subsistence. This concentration on one crop was symbolic of what was to happen to the economy of the whole Chesapeake Bay region in the generations to come. In spite of attempts by the government to encourage other crops, from the time of John Rolfe to the end of the eighteenth century Virginia depended exclusively on tobacco for its prosperity. Tobacco became the medium of exchange, and wages and salaries were calculated in so many pounds of tobacco. Even the parsons were paid in tobacco.

Robert Beverley in 1705, in *The History and Present State of Virginia,* complained that his fellow-countrymen concentrated so exclusively upon tobacco that they manufactured nothing for their own use, not even their woodenware; they ordered everything from merchants in London or Bristol and paid for these imports with tobacco shipped in English vessels, which anchored in the Virginia rivers and loaded their cargoes at the planters' own docks. The early explorers had not found gold, but the colonists had discovered a commodity that exceeded gold in its ultimate value.

The cultivation of tobacco was not without its problems. Greed resulted in overproduction and lower prices. By 1627 the price paid to the planter in Virginia had fallen to less than a penny a pound, and the Virginia Assembly in 1633 passed a law limiting each person who cultivated tobacco to fifteen hundred plants.[13] Thus we began governmental regulation of agricultural production, a practice that vexes us to this day.

The cultivation of tobacco required a great deal of hard labor. The young slips had to be transplanted from beds to the open fields when the danger of frost was past. The growing plants had to be hoed regularly to keep them from being smothered by grass and weeds. During the growing season it was necessary to go over the leaves regularly to pick off worms that would destroy them. In the late summer, when the leaves matured, the stalks were either cut or the leaves gathered in hanks and hung in barns for curing. Even yet the labor was not over, for when the tobacco was dried it had to be packed in hogsheads and rolled to the docks for loading. The necessity of ensuring sufficient labor for the tobacco fields, labor that required brawn rather than skill, made the purchase of African slaves attractive to planters in the Chesapeake Bay region. The conditions of tobacco cultivation made slavery profitable and helped to fasten this evil upon the tobacco-producing colonies.

During the seventeenth and eighteenth centuries tobacco production steadily increased, with periodic depressions in price. Since tobacco was the medium of exchange in the colonies producing it, fluctuating prices were always a serious problem affecting the welfare of the region. Various efforts were made by colonial governments to maintain some semblance of stability in prices, but their best endeavors were not always successful. The dynastic wars that disturbed the peace of Europe—and of the new world—throughout most of the eighteenth century curtailed the tobacco trade between England and the continent of Europe and thus reduced the price of raw tobacco in the colonies. But despite the fluctuations in price and the vicissitudes of trade in the colonial period, the cultivation of tobacco brought great wealth to Virginia, Maryland, and other regions where it could be grown. By the end of the colonial period, Virginia alone shipped an average of fifty thousand hogsheads of tobacco each year to Great Britain, worth approximately £500,000.[14] The processing and sale of tobacco products—smoking and chewing tobacco and snuff—also brought great wealth to merchants and manufacturers in both England and Scotland from the early eighteenth century onward.

The stimulation of the consumption of tobacco was a matter of great concern to growers, merchants, and processors, then as now. They were all eager to foster propaganda that would make people use more tobacco. Doctors and lay writers from time to time continued to publish commendations of tobacco and to refute heretics who charged that tobacco might be harmful. We shall see in the next few years whether the world has changed very radically in its attitude toward tobacco. William Byrd of Westover in Virginia, who took great pride in his membership in the Royal Society of London and fancied himself knowledgeable in medicine and science, wrote a treatise on the plague in 1721, which in the spring of that year he sent to London to be printed.[15] An anonymous pamphlet, entitled *A Discourse concerning the Plague with Some Preservatives against It, By a Lover of Mankind* (1721), is probably the one that Byrd wrote. It traces the history of the plague, enumerates various precautionary measures and treatments, and winds up with a resounding statement of the virtues of tobacco in warding off the pestilence.

The author is convinced that England and Holland have been spared plague epidemics since 1665 because of the rapid increase in the use of tobacco in those countries. Observers in London in 1665, he declares, reported that

> the houses of tobacco merchants and tobacconists who deal in large quantities of tobacco did wonderfully escape the infection. Nor are those colonies in America where they plant much tobacco ever visited with any distemper like the pestilence; but if by accident it has happened at any time to be carried thither by shipping, 'tis presently extinguished by the effluvia of this great antidote. . . . It has also been remarked that since the use of

tobacco has been so universal in Great Britain that all ranks of people either snuff, chew, or smoke, the plague has not paid us a visit half so often as formerly.[16]

The author emphasizes that the widespread use of tobacco among all degrees of people, "the rich as well as the poor, women as well as the men," has enormously improved the health of the English people. So much tobacco is consumed in London that he estimates "about the ninety-third part of the smoke that covers this great city must certainly be the smoke of tobacco. This it is that in probability purges our air and corrects those noisome damps that might otherwise beget contagious diseases amongst us." That a blanket of tobacco smog would preserve their health must have been a comfort to Londoners already suffering from the contamination of the air that remains such a problem for this metropolis.

As if this praise of tobacco would not suffice, the author concludes with specific advice to use more tobacco whenever infection threatens. "I am humbly of opinion," he declares,

> that when there is any danger of pestilence, we can't more effectually consult our preservation than by providing ourselves with a reasonable quantity of fresh, strong scented tobacco. We should wear it about our clothes and about our coaches. We should hang bundles of it around our beds and in the apartments wherein we most converse. If we have an aversion to smoking, it would be very prudent to burn some leaves of tobacco in our dining rooms lest we swallow infection with our meat. It will also be very useful to take snuff plentifully made of the pure leaf to secure the passages to our brain. Nor must those only be guarded, but the pass to our stomachs should be also defended by chewing this great anti-poison very frequently. . . . In short, we should both abroad and at home, by night as well as by day, alone and in company, take care to have our sovereign antidote very near us, an antidote which seems designed by Providence as the strongest natural preservative against this great destroyer.

From the time of Monardes to the day of William Byrd, from the naïve faith of the first explorers to the sophistication of the eighteenth-century virtuosi, tobacco was represented as a healer and a comforter of mankind. If the populace did not accept all of the claims of tobacco's advocates at face value, they at least felt secure in the use of the herb; in the course of time, tobacco became the universal solace of men—and of women—everywhere. Even now, when scientific investigation seems to prove that this weed is less than beneficent, millions of skeptics continue to puff their cigarettes and find comfort in their use. In the backwaters of America, many more men and women continue to believe in the therapeutic value of tobacco. Every countryman knows that for a bee or wasp sting a wet quid of chewing tobacco is a sovereign remedy. Folk beliefs die hard, even in an age of scientific research and television doctors.

The dream of a universal panacea still haunts mankind, and Americans today are hardly more sophisticated than their colonial ancestors. The Food and Drug Administration wages a constant campaign against worthless panaceas, ranging from pills to electronic devices. Vast fortunes are made from vitamins and other health-inducing products. No people in the world exceed Americans in the quantity of medical products consumed, and in no other country is the drug industry so profitable. Let it be said that the American drug industry has also accomplished many miracles for the relief of man's estate, and it is still conducting research that holds out hope that some at least of man's dreams of miracle cures may come true. *The New York Times* for February 2, 1964, carried a story of the development of an "all-purpose drug," something called "dimethyl sulfoxide or DMSO," which, says the report,

> has shown promise in getting other medicinal agents into the body, in killing pain, reducing inflammation, stopping the growth of bacteria, clearing the body of excess fluids, augmenting the beneficial effects of other medications, and in tranquilizing emotional distress. . . . The compound was also said to have

relieved post-surgical symptoms, sprains, and bruises, headaches, the common cold, sinusitis, and certain cases of arthritis.

All of these things, given a slight difference in terminology, Dr. Monardes promised four hundred years ago from the use of sassafras or tobacco. We still dream of cure-alls, and our yearnings fatten the dividends of many drug and chemical companies.

Notes

1. Evidently Dyer proved a satisfactory patron, because Frampton later translated and published other works dedicated to him: Marco Polo's *Travels* (1579), Bernardino de Escalante's *A Discourse of the Navigation which the Portugals Do Make to the Realms and Provinces of the East Parts of the World* (1579), and Pedro de Medina, *The Art of Navigation* (1581).
Frampton's *Joyful News* has been reprinted, with an introduction by Stephen Gaselee, in the Tudor Translations (2 vols., London, 1925). Citations are from this edition.

2. A discussion of the early literature on syphilis will be found in Fielding H. Garrison, *An Introduction to the History of Medicine,* 4th ed. (Philadelphia, 1960), pp. 190–91, 233. The name of the disease derives from a famous medical poem by Girolamo Fracastoro, *Syphilis sive Morbus Gallicus* (Venice, 1530).

3. Mary Newton Stanard, *The Story of Virginia's First Century* (Philadelphia, 1928), p. 40.

4. For the early history of tobacco and the literature on it, see Sarah Augusta Dickson, *Panacea or Precious Bane: Tobacco in Sixteenth Century Literature* (New York, 1954), *passim.* Concerning Hawkins, Raleigh, and other early users of tobacco in England, see pp. 131 ff.

5. *Ibid.,* p. 132.

6. *Ibid.,* p. 44.

7. *Ibid.,* p. 98.

8. *Ibid.,* p. 103.

9. James E. Gillespie, *The Influence of Oversea Expansion on England to 1700* (New York, 1820), pp. 83–84.

10. Dickson, *Panacea or Precious Bane,* p. 104.

11. *Ibid.,* p. 196.

12. Richard L. Morton, *Colonial Virginia* (2 vols., Chapel Hill, N.C., 1960), I, 39–44, 93–96.

13. *Ibid.,* I, 132–33.

14. *Ibid.,* II, 824.

15. Byrd tells in his diary of writing his treatise on the plague and of sending it to London to be printed. See *The London Diary (1717–1721) and Other Writings of William Byrd,* edited by Louis B. Wright and Marion Tinling (New York, 1958), entries for Feb. 14, 20, 24; March 16, 22, 26; April 8, 1721.

16. *Another Secret Diary of William Byrd of Westover, 1739–1741,* edited by Maude H. Woodfin and Marion Tinling (Richmond, Va., 1942), pp. 439–43.

IV

The Continuing Dream of
an Economic Utopia

THE economic planners in London, personified in the members
of the Board of Trade and Plantations, sometimes called the Lords
of Trade, and the North American colonists, busily hewing out
commonwealths along the Atlantic seaboard, never gave up their
dreams of finding fresh sources of prosperity in the new world.
Even the humblest indentured servant looked forward to his freedom, when he might take up land and become the proprietor of
his own estate. The great men sitting around their council tables
in London were hoping for the day when the colonies overseas
would produce all of the products that England now bought from
her rivals and the realm could become a vast self-contained empire.

The combined zeal of the ruling authorities and the eager colonists ought to have produced this economic Utopia, but unfortunately
the aims of the Londoners and the interests of the colonists did not
always coincide, and the best laid plans of the mercantilists often
went awry. The colonists frequently proved contrary, obstinate, and
perversely oblivious to theories about a closed protectionist empire.
In short, they were ruled by self-interest; and self-interest often
made smugglers and tax chiselers out of pious Puritans and godly
Quakers. Furthermore, the Lords of Trade almost invariably

thought first of the good of England and only secondarily about the welfare of farmers and fishermen on the other side of the Atlantic. Thus, while everyone was struggling toward the mirage of an economic paradise, notions of how to attain this blissful state varied widely and these differences caused increasing dissension as the years went by.

But economic planning in London was not without its rewards, both for England and for her colonies. Substantial opinion now holds that the Navigation Acts, frequently represented by American historians as unmitigated instruments for the oppression of the colonies, actually served a useful purpose, not only for the people of England but for the colonists as well.[1]

Be that as it may, the colonists themselves did not take kindly to the Navigation Acts and exerted great ingenuity in circumventing them. From the Act of 1651 until the Revolution, Parliament passed law after law designed to funnel into English ports all of the most important colonial raw materials, which had to be conveyed in ships bearing the English flag. As the years went by the "enumerated articles"—those products that could only be shipped to English ports in English-flag vessels—continued to increase until they included almost everything except fish and barrel staves. Furthermore, if the colonists wanted to import goods from a foreign country, such goods had to be landed first in England and a duty paid on them before they were transhipped to the colonies in English-flag vessels. All of this added to the price of manufactured goods from foreign countries and tended to make the colonies dependent upon English manufactures, which was the purpose behind the laws.

It is small wonder that ship captains from Boston, Philadelphia, and other colonial ports contrived to rendezvous with French, Dutch, and Spanish ships conveniently fishing off Newfoundland and to trade tobacco and other enumerated products for brandy, wine, silk goods, and other foreign luxuries. They also managed to develop a thriving trade in contraband sugar and molasses from the non-British islands of the West Indies. American merchants, particularly those of New England, were achieving prosperity, but they were not proceeding exactly as the Lords of Trade had intended.

The colonies that came nearest to meeting the ideal specifications of the economic planners' dreams were Virginia and Maryland, and the product that made this happy condition possible was of course tobacco. Here was a commodity that in its raw state brought a profit to the growers; shipped to England and processed there it made work for English laborers, brought wealth to English merchants, and provided through duties and taxes a never-ending source of revenue for the government.

The only fly in this mercantilist ointment was the fact that the tobacco-growing colonies in good years could produce more tobacco than the mother country could consume and the price would sink so low that Virginia, Maryland, and other producers could not purchase a desirable quantity of British goods. The concentration upon tobacco also hindered the production of other commodities that the mother country needed, especially raw silk, dyestuffs, wines, and luxury foods such as dates, raisins, and figs. Furthermore, late in the seventeenth century, when the price of tobacco sank, small farmers, who had only the labor of their own hands and the help of their families, found it difficult to grow enough tobacco to keep soul and body together. Only the great planters with gangs of African slaves could make a profit from tobacco. Tobacco also exhausted the soil after about seven years, and many small growers had to abandon their worn-out tobacco fields and seek their fortunes on the frontier, where fresh land could be had for subsistence farming. This early movement to the interior stimulated an interest in land to the west, an interest that would in time become an overwhelming mania of fortune seekers. Thus early, Americans developed a habit of restless mobility that has become one of our most characteristic traits.

Like tobacco, sugar production was an answer to the mercantilists' prayers, for raw sugar, produced with slave labor in the British West Indies, could be shipped to England for refining and then sold at a handsome profit both at home and abroad. Also like tobacco, sugar was at first recommended for its medicinal values. The seventeenth-century herbalists regarded sugar cane as a medicinal plant, and more than three hundred medicines prescribed in the seventeenth century used sugar as an important ingredient. One learned doctor was fond of quoting a verse: "If sugar can preserve both pears and plums,/Why can it not preserve as well the lungs?" [2] Perhaps the notion that sugar is a preservative accounts for the frequent use of sugar in the sweetened meat dishes that our seventeenth-century ancestors managed to eat.

A by-product of sugar making is molasses, which also found a favored place as a preservative of health; it too was used as an ingredient in many medicines. Even today, health faddists promise infinite good things if one will only adopt a diet of blackstrap molasses. A further by-product of the sugar industry was rum, which helped to transform American civilization, as we shall presently see. The sugar islands in the West Indies, therefore, held out the promise of great wealth, and Englishmen flocked to reap profits from sugar cane grown with slave labor.

The island of Barbados turned out to be the sugar paradise of British America and almost the perfect example of the mercantilists' notion of the ideal relationship between colony and mother country. The development of the island's economy to this ideal state was not accomplished without trial and stress.[3] First settled in 1625, the island was long a bone of contention between London merchants, the proprietors who had received the grant of the island, and the great planters on the island itself, who managed to achieve quasi-independence in the early years of the Puritan Revolution. Eventually Barbados emerged as a crown colony and one of the richest producers of sugar in the West Indies. Sugar supplanted tobacco as a staple commodity in Barbados in the 1640's, and by 1650 it was called the "soul of trade." By the end of the seventeenth century, Barbados was shipping to Great Britain each year sugar valued at between £200,000 and £300,000 sterling. Britain's exports of merchantable commodities to Barbados amounted to something like half this amount.[4] But, as in Virginia, the glut of the market frequently brought the price down so that the small growers were hard pressed to make a profit. Gradually the smaller planters sold out and emigrated and the larger planters consolidated their holdings until eventually Barbados was a series of immense sugar plantations, operated by slave labor and owned by lordly grandees, some of whom were absentees. Many of the early settlers in South Carolina were Barbadian emigrés who deemed it wiser to seek their fortunes on the mainland than to compete with the great sugar magnates on the island. As it ultimately developed, paradise on Barbados was for the few. In 1684 the island had approximately 20,000 white inhabitants and 46,000 slaves, and as the years went on the proportion of black slaves to white inhabitants increased.

Sugar, like tobacco, proved to be a commodity of immense profit to British merchants. By 1675, the trade between England and the West Indies had increased to a point where approximately 400 merchant ships averaging 150 tons burden were required each year to transport sugar and molasses to Great Britain. So great was Britain's concern about sugar that nearly a century later, at the Peace of Paris in 1763, she was ready to allow France to retain all of Canada in exchange for the single West Indian sugar island of Guadeloupe. This deal might have been consummated if British owners of sugar plantations had not protested that the addition of the French sugar island would ruin their market for raw sugar.

The production of sugar and molasses in the West Indies proved a boon of enormous value to the British colonies on the mainland of North America, especially to the New England colonies, where shipbuilding and fishing were major industries. The New Englanders discovered that the West Indies provided a ready market for barrel staves and cooperage of all sorts, since sugar and molasses had to be shipped in hogsheads. Because the islanders were preoccupied with one crop, they needed to import foodstuffs, which the mainlanders were ready to supply. It was not long before the New Englanders also perceived that huge profits could be made by distilling West Indian molasses into rum, which was highly prized on the coast of Africa, where it could be traded for slaves, gold dust, and ivory. Slaves were eagerly sought for the burgeoning sugar plantations, and godly New England ship captains were glad to bring back cargoes of heathen to a country of Christians where they might exchange their lifelong labor for Christian baptism and the hope of heaven. Many a slave trader, including Peter Faneuil of Boston, salved his conscience in this fashion and happily pocketed his profits.

Rum found its earnest advocates, although it earned the name of "kill-devil" with others. Some who commended rum pointed out that rum drinkers lived to a ripe old age, whereas brandy drinkers died young.[5] Since brandy was imported from France, and rum originated within the closed protectionist empire, the propaganda in favor of rum might be suspect. Even yet a latent distrust of French brandy can be found in British folk belief. I once had a cockney housekeeper in London who, on discovering a bottle of cognac in my cupboard, earnestly warned that it might be mortal. "Brandy-drinkin' and eatin' of tinned foods is very un'ealthy," she declared. Not all Englishmen were happy about the rum tide. British gin distillers regarded rum as an evil, but they were unable to dam the flood or even to keep rum from finding an honored place in naval rations. Rum had come to stay and to enrich both colonial and British producers.

By trial and error the British colonies at length discovered ways of attaining prosperity, not always to the liking of the home government. For example, New England for the most part aroused the suspicion and sometimes the outright wrath of the Lords of Trade by competing with British industries and refusing to promote those trades and commodities useful to England. Perversely, the colonies developed an iron and steel industry. In Virginia, Governor Spotswood himself was known as the Tubal-cain of the colony because of his interest in iron mines. New Englanders operated iron mines, forges, and slitting mills, and produced bar iron and steel of excellent quality. Furthermore, because of the inexhaustible supply of wood for charcoal, iron and steel could be manufactured in America cheaper than in Britain. So hateful was this competition that Parliament passed the Iron Act in 1750, prohibiting the erection in America of any more slitting or steel mills. The act encouraged the production of pig and bar iron destined for shipment to Great Britain. But like many other prohibitory laws, the Iron Act was more honored in the breach than the observance, and American iron foundries continued to produce to such an extent that their total output by the time of the Revolution was greater than that of England and Wales.[6]

Another industry that brought prosperity to colonial Americans and caused envy and unhappiness among competitors in England was shipbuilding. The very conditions of the Navigation Act of 1660 served to spur the shipbuilding industry in America, for this act specified that ships bearing the British merchant flag must be of British or colonial origin. From the 1630's New England shipyards had been turning out seaworthy vessels, and their production increased after 1660. Since oak was plentiful and pines and firs for masts and spars were easily available, ships could be built at a smaller cost over here than in England. By the end of the colonial period, Great Britain was buying from her American colonies something like 30 percent of the total number of vessels engaged in her commerce.[7]

Worse than this, the industrious New Englanders were encroaching on Britain's carrying trade and fisheries. Since colonial vessels could fly the British merchant flag and were entitled to the privileges of other British ships, the Navigation Acts could not prevent this encroachment. By the Revolution, three-fourths of the goods shipped from the North American colonies were carried in vessels owned by colonials. So numerous were the American vessels engaged in the fisheries that the British feared that their own fishermen would be driven from Newfoundland waters by New England's competition. By 1771 more than a thousand New England vessels were engaged in fishing and whaling.[8] Farming the seas and using the seas as a highway for commerce brought continuing prosperity to New England and persistent apprehension to the Lords of Trade in London, whose business it was to worry about the health of British shipping.

Although the economic planners were frequently disappointed over the poor results of their attempts to stimulate the production of particular commodities, they did not relax their efforts to stir laggard colonials to labor for the good of the protectionist empire. For example, from the beginning to the end of the colonial period the English government strove to induce colonials to produce raw silk. The silk delusion was one of the most persistent notions that plagued official London. The planners never gave up the hope that eventually, if they offered sufficient inducements and instructions, somewhere the colonists would become silk producers and thus save a vast tide of money that flowed out of England every year to pay for the silk that fashion demanded.

As we have seen, King James I believed that all the Jamestown settlers needed to become silk growers was a book of directions equipped with a royal preface by himself; but Jamestown failed him. A letter dated May 27, 1621, from Captain Thomas Nuce to Sir Edwin Sandys, secretary of the Virginia Company of London, has a postscript that explains why the silk venture failed in Virginia —and why it would continue to fail in all of the colonies. The people who made trial of the silkworm eggs previously sent over are now much discouraged, Nuce declares. The price of silk cocoons (which Nuce calls cods) is only two shillings, sixpence per pound, and that is not enough to enable a man to grow silkworms in a country where the cost of labor is high. "But I would be glad to understand," Nuce asserts,

> by those merchants who value the cods at two shillings, sixpence a pound, when this will prove a commodity for men to live by in this country where we pay three shillings a day for the labor of a man who hath no other way but to dig and delve. Sure[ly] they thought themselves in Italy, Spain, or France, countries plentiful and populous, where are thousands of women and

children and such idle people to be hired for one penny or two pennies a day.[9]

Nuce adds that silkworms require care during the same season when corn needs cultivation, "so as no man but he that means to starve will once look after them."

The high cost of labor was the rock upon which the silk venture invariably wrecked, but apparently the colonial authorities in London never learned, or refused to concede the truth of this observation, for they continued to promote silk production for a century and a half after Jamestown.

Perhaps one reason for their persistence was the knowledge that the Spaniards had successfully introduced silk culture into the new world. Curiously, an early Spanish project for silk culture fixed upon the North Carolina coast as the place for its establishment. In 1521 Lúcas Vásquez de Ayllón had explored the region and two years later received permission from the Spanish crown to settle a colony on the Cape Fear River. He had held out a promise that he would bring over skilled workers in silk, with a supply of silkworm eggs, and would train the Indians, whom he would subjugate, in the peaceful craft of silk making. In 1625 Ayllón actually landed a colony of 200 Spaniards, but they eventually became discouraged, abandoned their habitations, and sailed for Santo Domingo. The Cape Fear Indians were not sufficiently tractable to become raisers of silkworms, and it is doubtful whether Allyón's silk specialists ever hatched a silkworm egg in North Carolina.[10] But his project is worth remembering because of later efforts by the English to make silk raising a profitable enterprise in the Carolinas and Georgia.

The knowledge that the Spaniards had successfully introduced silk growing in Mexico was undoubtedly an influence upon English promoters, for the Mexican venture had been sensational. For a time in the mid-sixteenth century, silk raising in Mexico rivaled gold mining in profits. Mexican Indians learned to handle the silkworms and to reel the silk from cocoons. By the 1540's, silk growing had reached the proportions of a boom and had spread through much of Mexico. Observers of the rapid growth of the Mexican silk industry predicted that Mexico would rival Spain and Italy in silk production. Although the industry later suffered a severe backset, the Spaniards had proved that silk could be grown profitably in the new world. What the Spaniards could do, surely Englishmen could emulate. At least they would not fail for lack of stimulation from the home government.

Throughout the colonial period, authorities in London continued to advocate silk culture as a certain means of ensuring prosperity to the inhabitants of America; but of more concern to these officials was the hope that silk from the colonies would stop the flow of gold that poured into foreign silk markets. By the last quarter of the eighteenth century, England was spending £500,000 annually on Chinese silk.[11]

Because of their mild climate, the colonies of the Deep South held out the greatest promise for silk culture, and it was there that the promoters made their most vigorous attempts to establish the industry.

Sir Nathaniel Johnson, one of the prominent planters of South Carolina at the end of the seventeenth century and governor from 1703 to 1709, tried with some success to raise silk; a gift of raw silk that he sent to the lord proprietors in 1699 encouraged them to believe that the industry was in a promising state. Sir Nathaniel significantly named his own plantation "Silk Hope." Although South Carolina had the benefit of skilled French Huguenot craftsmen, some of whom were trained in silk production, and although some silk, described as being equal to any produced in Italy or France, was shipped to England in the eighteenth century, the industry failed. But it did not fail without diligent effort. As late as 1772, a Swiss settlement at Purrysburgh on the Savannah River was still struggling to make silk and was exporting a few hundred pounds each year.

The settlement of Georgia once more held a promise of a great silk industry, as well as hope for the production of all the exotic products that had come to nought in the other colonies. Georgia was to be a new Eden, producing all the good things that man might require. In 1732 a group of trustees comprising General James Oglethorpe, the Earl of Egmont, and nineteen other prominent Englishmen, received a charter and the grant of a tract of land "southwest of Carolina for settling poor persons of London." This was to be a charitable as well as a profitable enterprise, and indigent debtors might rehabilitate themselves by making silk on the banks of the Savannah River. The seal of the trustees bore a design of busy silkworms surrounded by the motto *Non Sibi Sed Aliis.*[12] The trustees' original plan provided that each indigent person coming to Georgia should receive a life tenure in fifty acres of land, provided that he cleared ten acres and planted one hundred mulberry trees.[13] Those who came at their own expense would receive land at the rate of fifty acres per white adult. Such independent "adventurers" were required to plant 1,000 mulberry trees for each 100 acres in their grants.

A group of refugee Lutherans from Salzburg found a haven in Georgia and began silk production. By 1735 they had made enough silk to send a parcel to England, where it was presented to the queen, who had it made into a dress. By 1750 those Salzburgers were producing more than 1,000 pounds of cocoons each year. Others were also making silk, and a silk-winding works in Savannah in 1764 received 15,000 pounds of cocoons. Oglethorpe's mulberry trees were bearing fruit. In the meantime, the trustees had sent experts to Madeira, the West Indies, and South America to search for exotic plants, fruit trees, vines, and herbs that might enrich the new Eden.

But Georgia, like the other colonies, turned out to be a disappointment. The silk works declined as grosser commodities like rice and naval stores proved more profitable. The olive and the date palm refused to grow. And the keepers of vineyards were somehow unable to produce wine in commercial quantities or to dry raisins in the humid summer climate. Georgia obstinately declined to become a tropical paradise.

But promoters of silk culture remained convinced to the very last that this was an industry of tremendous value to the colonists themselves as well as to the mother country. An anonymous author who in 1775 published in London a two-volume work entitled *American Husbandry* devoted many pages to advocating the growing of silk. With neat logic he demonstrated that silk could be easily and profitably made in most of the settled areas of British North America. The identity of the author has puzzled bibliographers, and no satisfactory answer has been found. The original title page simply said "By an American," but whoever wrote the book expressed the favorite ideas of the English mercantilists. The colonies that were already shipping profitable raw materials to England received high praise for these products, but the author exhorts them to consider the potential profits from those other items that the English market still required.

The author of *American Husbandry* displays an almost desperate eagerness to encourage the production of both wine and silk, the two commodities that were costing Great Britain the heaviest outlays in cash. In discussing the various colonies from north to south, he considers their potentiality for both silk and wine. Most of the colonies could produce these commodities, he thinks, if they would only show a little more ingenuity and initiative.

The Pennsylvanians' "inattention to vines is very inexcusable," he asserts, and he indicates that their failure to make silk is evidence of sheer perversity: "The people do not in the least pretend that the climate is improper; their only argument is that the price of labor is too high." [14] This argument he refutes by showing that silk making

> is a work executed at a certain season of the year, which lasts only for six weeks, by the females of the family, by the young and aged that cannot perform laborious work. . . . Nothing can therefore be more absurd than to urge the high price of labor as a reason why silk cannot be made in this province. Labor is yet dearer in Georgia, but silk is there made in large quantities.

Yet even as he wrote, silk making in Georgia was a dying industry for the very reason that he was trying to refute.

To the author of *American Husbandry,* Virginia and Maryland were particularly disappointing because they had neglected silk culture. "None of our colonies enjoy a climate so well adapted to the purpose," he delares.

> Mulberry trees are found everywhere in profusion, and the work of winding the silk and attending the worms might be carried on without any material interruption of their tobacco culture; but the advantage of making silk is its being in a great measure proper for uniting with almost any business, since women, old infirm persons, and even children make as good a figure in it as the most robust men, a point of vast consequence.[15]

The author maintains that the tobacco colonies, with 800,000 inhabitants ought to average each season at least a pound of silk for every inhabitant. "But if only 500,000 pounds were made, it would add exceedingly to the wealth of both Britain and the colony," he remarks somewhat pensively.

North and South Carolina, the author insists, should be great producers of both silk and wine, and he argues that only lack of initiative has kept them from making sound profits from these commodities. Georgia had obtained a vast tract of land from the Cherokees in 1761, and here at last would be the Eden that would produce the scarce commodities that the empire still needed, the author of *American Husbandry* decided. "It is very much to be wished that so fine a tract of country may be put to the most advantageous use, particularly in respect of silk, wine, and hemp," he asserts.

> These are commodities which we want more than any others from our colonies, but for want of a proper soil and climate the nation [Great Britain] has for so many years been disappointed in its expectations; but there can be no doubt of all these articles doing as well in this newly acquired country as in any part of

the world, provided the right methods are taken in the culture of them.[16]

But, alas for the mercantilists, logic, even so persuasively stated as in the arguments of the author of *American Husbandry,* did not influence farmers in any of the colonies. They had no concern about the prosperity of the empire. They were concerned with those crops that they could grow most easily and turn into ready money or its equivalent in usable goods. Silk, wine, and hemp—products so eagerly desired of the American colonies by London—went down before tobacco, rice, and indigo in the colonies of the Deep South.

The planners in Whitehall could never see why the other desired commodities could not be grown in addition to the ones that the colonists favored. They simply reckoned without any consideration of human nature and of the special conditions prevailing in the colonies overseas. A program that looked simple to a planner in London might prove insuperable to a planter living in the humid swamps of South Carolina or Georgia. These practical men on the ground put their faith in commodities that they knew they could produce. The price of experimentation might be bankruptcy and disaster.

Yet unconsciously the planters helped to fit their production programs into the mercantilists' scheme of things. For example, until the colonies began to produce indigo in quantity in the eighteenth century, Great Britain had been forced to buy blue dye from her enemies. But by 1748 South Carolina alone was exporting indigo worth £16,764. In the same year the colony's rice exports amounted to £88,600. By 1754, the exports of indigo were worth £27,115 and the rice exports had climbed to £183,193. Deerskins—used for fine leather clothing, breeches, jackets, and gloves—also proved desirable; by 1754 the export of skins amounted to £23,000.[17] Even if the colonies did not serve all of the requirements of the mercantilists, they were supplying substantial quantities of commodities that made it unnecessary for Great Britain to purchase these products from foreign competitors.

One item that proved as elusive as silk, wine, and hemp was the red dyestuff cochineal, which the British needed for their military uniforms.

Several planters in east Florida late in the colonial period tried to produce cochineal, among other products, but they failed. Cochineal consists of tiny dried insects, the *Coccus cacti,* that flourish on cacti indigenous to Mexico and the Caribbean.[18] The planters in Florida lost money trying to raise the insects, and Great Britain continued to buy cochineal, either directly or indirectly from Spain. Thus the red dye that went into British military uniforms and made the wearers such excellent targets ironically had to be obtained from one of Britain's most ancient enemies.

Although, as the author of *American Husbandry* indicates in his description of agriculture, the colonies had often disappointed the mother country, by the end of the first quarter of the eighteenth century the successes far outweighed the disappointments. Great Britain was growing richer by the year from North American raw materials and from finished products sold to overseas inhabitants.

This was a period of speculation, when greed for money had taken possession of many men with a force greater than the normal avarice of humankind. In 1711 the South Sea Company was organized by Robert Harley to trade with South America and the islands of the Pacific. Dreams of the profits to be made in this trade lured investors to bid up the stock, which rose spectacularly until the value of shares multiplied ten times. In the meanwhile other companies were organized, some with fantastic objectives, until finally in 1720 the South Sea Bubble burst, ruining thousands of investors.

But the wreck of the South Sea Company and of other similar schemes did not cure investors of a desire to get rich overnight. The virus of speculation was in the blood and it spread to America. All sorts of plans were hatched for discovering economic Utopias in America. The riches that many British investors had already drawn from the new world made others think that anything might be possible in the vast and mysterious continent overseas. The colonials themselves were also convinced that riches could be had from the acquisition of land, and their land hunger knew no bounds. Land speculation became a dominant characteristic of American life in the early eighteenth century and it gathered momentum as the years went by.

Some of the more colorful schemes to get land and to establish new Edens in America were dreamed up by Scots intent upon improving their fortunes.[19] Perhaps the best known is the plan of Sir Robert Montgomery of Skelmorly to create a colony in what is now Georgia and Alabama fifteen years before Oglethorpe succeeded in his endeavor. Montgomery set forth his scheme in a promotional tract entitled *A Discourse concerning the Designed Establishment of a New Colony to the South of Carolina in the Most Delightful Country of the Universe* (1717).[20] Montgomery gave the name of Azilia to the territory, described it as "our future Eden," and announced that "Paradise with all her virgin beauties may be modestly supposed at most but equal to its native excellencies." Montgomery showed himself a true mercantilist by promising to produce "coffee, tea, figs, raisins, currants, almonds, olives, silk, wine, cochineal, and a great variety of still more rich commodities which we are [now] forced to buy at mighty rates from countries lying in the very latitude of our plantation." And, lest any prospective settler might worry about what he would live on while waiting for the development of these products, Montgomery airily assured readers of his tract that at first the colonists would confine themselves to "such easy benefits as will without the smallest waiting for the growth of plants be offered to our industry from the spontaneous wealth which overruns the country." The notion of spontaneous wealth overrunning the country had been the delusion that wrecked many an earlier colonial venture, but Montgomery was spared the actual experience of searching for this wealth when the whole plan blew up in the depression that followed the collapse of the South Sea Bubble.

An even wilder scheme, however, was devised by another Scottish baronet, Sir Alexander Cuming of Coulter, who, with humanitarian zeal, conceived the notion of helping the oppressed Jews of Europe by creating a Zion among the Cherokee Indians in the back country of South Carolina. What the Cherokees thought of donating tribal land for the 300,000 Jews that Cuming proposed to send over is not recorded. Nor is it recorded that these oppressed people themselves were privy to Cuming's benign plan to move them to the mountains of South Carolina. Meanwhile, however, Cuming in 1730 made a pilgrimage to the Cherokee country, persuaded some of the Cherokees to kneel and swear allegiance to King George, and a few months afterward returned to London with seven Indians, whom he presented at court as a king and six great chiefs. They created a sensation, were lionized and spoiled, and eventually were restored to their astonished tribesmen in South Carolina. But Cuming's emigration scheme for oppressed Jews came to nothing.[21]

Still another Scot, Archibald Menzies of Megerny Castle, Perthshire, decided in 1763 that, since Florida had become an English possession, it could be made another Eden producing exotic commodities that had eluded previous colonizers. He proposed to find emigrants who understood the mystery of raising olives, grapes, and silkworms, and he decided that the best people for the purpose would be Greeks, Minorcans, and Armenians. Although nothing came of his plan, another Scot, Dr. Andrew Turnbull, in 1767 actually succeeded in settling some Greeks, Minorcans, and Italians at New Smyrna on the east coast below St. Augustine. But this colony proved as unsuccessful as all the other schemes as a source of exotic products beneficial to the British empire.

Within the colonies themselves a restlessness to move on to greener pastures was characteristic of many of the settlers. By the mid-eighteenth century, pioneers were pushing beyond the settled areas and probing the mountain barriers. But long before this time a few daring traders and adventurers had begun the gradual movement westward that would accelerate with the passing years.

The realities of life in the early settlements had long since dimmed the rosy dreams of terrestrial paradises where food would rain like manna upon the happy colonists. Forests stood like a dark wall beyond the clearings, and behind that wall bloodthirsty savages might lie in wait for the unwary. Settlers who had gained a foothold on the seaboard and perhaps had achieved a modicum of prosperity were little inclined to talk about their holdings as new Edens. Such descriptions were more usual in the mouths of promoters of colonization. But the settlers themselves were no less convinced that prosperity would eventually crown their efforts. Optimism has been characteristic of the American from the beginning.

But the optimism of the experienced settlers was somewhat different from that of the armchair travelers and writers about America. The settlers' faith in their future was based on observation and experience and a realistic appraisal of the opportunities awaiting the courageous and the diligent. Instead of believing that the new land was a Garden of Eden, Puritan colonists even came to regard the unsettled areas as a howling wilderness of evil, peopled with demons, to try the souls of God's saints.[22] When at last they had overcome the hardships of the wilderness, driven back the Indians, and transformed the desert into a garden, it was proof of their election as the favored people of the Almighty.

The sense of being the chosen people was transformed into a doctrine of manifest destiny, a belief that had an early beginning in this country. The Puritans were certain that they had a destiny to wrest the wilderness from the demons who inhabited it and to make it over into a garden of the Lord for the use of His elect. The Puritans of New England and the Presbyterian Scots who came later often quoted a text from Joshua (13:1): "And there remaineth yet very much land to be possessed." They interpreted this passage as a charter straight from the Bible to move into the wilderness, to smite the Canaanites, and to seize the good land that pleased them. And that is precisely what they frequently did. A few, a very few, still talked of converting the Indians to the Christian faith.

From an early date the lure of western land proved irresistible. In the summer of 1650, Edward Bland, an English merchant resident in Virginia, and Abraham Wood, a militia captain and Indian trader, led an expedition from the site of Petersburg to a point in southwest Virginia where they discovered a river which they believed ran west. The next year Bland printed in London *The Discovery of New Britain* (1651), which carried a preface praising the land and urging all who desired "the advancement of God's glory by the conversion of the Indians [and] the augmentation of the English commonwealth in extending its liberties" to consider "the present benefit and future profits" of settling the new territory lying between thirty-five and thirty-seven degrees north latitude.

This geographical position had a mystical significance, for Raleigh had pointed out that God had placed Eden on the thirty-fifth parallel of north latitude, and Bland's tract reprinted the passage describing Eden from Raleigh's *Marrow of History*.[23] Bland, like Raleigh before him, believed that this location guaranteed an ideal climate and a garden-like land, perhaps wooded with palm trees, described by Raleigh as the greatest blessing and wonder of nature. Although Bland exhorted readers of his book to help him claim this wilderness paradise, the time was not yet ripe for emigration into the interior, and only a few adventurers took advantage of the suggestion.

Gradually Indian traders pushed into lands beyond the first mountain ranges. The first William Byrd late in the seventeenth century sent pack trains with trade goods into the back country of Virginia and Carolina. A rival trader, Abraham Wood, from his base at Petersburg, also penetrated the interior. No one knows the name of the first Englishman who crossed the Alleghenies and discovered the Ohio Valley. The earliest written record of the penetration from Virginia of this portion of the West is a journal kept by Robert Fallam, who, along with Captain Thomas Batts and Thomas Wood, passed the divide on September 13, 1671, and drank out of a tributary of the Ohio River. But as they explored the river valley they came upon trees marked with initials of previous adventurers.

Abraham Wood, Byrd's rival in the fur trade, was instrumental in promoting the Batts-Fallam-Wood expedition. In the meantime Byrd himself was directing the exploration of the same territory, but how far west his agents went no one knows. When Batts and his colleagues were returning, they met Indians near the crest of the mountains who gave them "the news of Mr. Byrd and his great company's discoveries three miles from the Tetera's town." [24] Competition for western land and for profits from the Indian trade had already begun in 1671.

Fallam wrote in his journal that the land was exceedingly rich and promising. He also reported that he saw in a westerly direction "over a certain delightful hill a fog arise and a glimmering light as from water. We supposed there to be a great bay" [25]—an arm of the South Sea. As for Batts, he thought he saw sails upon the water. The illusion of a westerly passage to the Pacific and to the islands of spices still persisted.

Fallam's journal was copied by the Reverend John Clayton, parson at Jamestown, and sent to the Royal Society in London, of which Clayton was a corresponding member. It excited the interest of the learned members of that body. About 1687 a second copy of the journal was made for Dr. Daniel Coxe, another member of the Royal Society and a notable advocate of western expansion. Dr. Coxe, prominent physician and scientist, used the journal as the basis of an argument to the Board of Trade that the West ought to be colonized by Englishmen.

The most picturesque and best known of the early explorations from Virginia was the celebrated expedition led by Governor Alexander Spotswood across the Blue Ridge Mountains in September, 1716. Accompanied by the historian Robert Beverley, John Fontaine—a Huguenot gentleman who kept a journal—and a party of about fifty men, Spotswood discovered the Shenandoah River, which he named the Euphrates after one of the four rivers of Eden. Fontaine's journal, the chief source of information about these explorations, provides a fascinating account of one of the most convivial expeditions on record. Fontaine reports an incredible consumption of liquor and frequent encounters with rattlesnakes of an appalling size. Whether there is any connection between these facts a historian at this late date cannot say. On September 5 Fontaine writes: "We drank King George's health, and all the Royal Family's, at the very top of the Appalachian mountains. . . . I being somewhat more curious than the rest, went on a high rock on the top of the mountain, to see fine prospects, and I lost my gun." The next day, Spotswood buried an empty bottle containing a paper saying that he took possession of the region in the name of George I, King of England. At the conclusion of this ceremony, says Fontaine,

> We had a good dinner, and after it we got the men together, and loaded all their arms, and we drank the King's health in champagne, and fired a volley; the Princess' health in burgundy, and fired a volley; and all the rest of the royal family in claret, and fired a volley. We drank the Governor's health and fired another volley: We had several sorts of liquors, viz., Virginia red wine and white wine, Irish usquebaugh, brandy, shrub, two sorts of rum, champagne, canary, cherry punch, water, cider, etc.[26]

Spotswood memorialized the journey by creating the "Transmontane Order" and presenting his companions with golden horseshoes "to encourage gentlemen to venture backwards and make discoveries and new settlements," says Hugh Jones, a contemporary historian.[27]

Great as was the speculative interest of Virginia gentlemen in the western lands, the actual settlement of the interior was the labor of other people. By the end of the seventeenth century, the push westward had begun all along the Atlantic seaboard. From the time of Roger Williams onward, Puritans who found themselves in disagreement with the rigorous authorities of Massachusetts Bay bettered their lot by moving out of the Bay's jurisdiction—into Rhode Island, into the Connecticut Valley, into New Hampshire, into western New York, into the wilds of Pennsylvania. New England's westward expansion—unlike that in the colonies to the south—was frequently a community enterprise. Whole congregations, under the leadership of a preacher or of pious laymen, removed to territory where they could set up the sort of church polity which best suited them.

In the far South, cattle raisers and farmers pushed into the up country from Charleston, South Carolina, until they reached the foothills. By the beginning of the eighteenth century, Indian traders from Charleston had penetrated the mountains and reached the country of the Cherokees, the Creeks, and the Chickasaws. By 1700 Carolina adventurers had crossed the Mississippi River.

Western expansion, however, would have remained for many years a spasmodic movement, confined to the activities of Indian traders and adventurous speculators, or to religious groups from New England, had it not been for the mass migration to America of the Scotch-Irish from Ulster and the Germans from the Rhineland. A few Scots and a somewhat larger number of Germans had arrived in this country before 1700, but the great tide of immigration began after the turn of the century and continued for the remainder of the colonial period.

William Penn's propaganda advertising the virtues of his proprietary colony of Pennsylvania aroused the interest of Germans and Scots. As early as 1683, Francis Daniel Pastorius, a lawyer of Frankfort, led a group of Pietists from the lower Rhine to Philadelphia. Pennsylvania, with its promise of peace and prosperity, appealed to these people, who had suffered incredibly from the recurrent wars which swept the Rhine country. William Penn promised them fertile soil in a Quaker land which hated war. The earliest Germans were Mennonites and pacifists of related sects. Many of them were craftsmen and skilled workers. A few, like the leader, Pastorius, were learned men. During the early years of the eighteenth century a new type of German began to arrive in Pennsylvania. These Germans were for the most part Lutherans of peasant stock and were generally "redemptioners"—that is, they sold themselves into bondage for a period of years, usually a five-year term, to pay their passage over. They had little interest in learning, but they were the most skillful farmers this country had seen. The first Germans settled near Philadelphia, but later arrivals pushed onward into the back country. Penn's treaties with the Indians made possible the peaceful occupation of interior lands, which the Germans soon made as productive as garden plots.

The Scotch-Irish also read Penn's advertisements of a country which promised an abundance of rich land and freedom from interference in any man's religion. No combination of promises could have been more appealing to the Scots of Ulster. They had left the lowlands of Scotland to occupy the confiscated farms of Catholics in Northern Ireland. Though they had multiplied, they had found neither prosperity nor liberty there. They felt that the English government had dealt hardly with them. Restrictive laws on the export of Irish woolens caused hardships to the Ulster weavers. Exorbitant rents imposed by English landlords aroused deep resentment. And worst of all, the Test Act of 1704 excluded from every military and civil office Scots who did not become communicants of the established church of Ireland. This effort of the Church of England to root out dissent among Scotch-Irish Protestants convinced many Ulstermen that their only hope of religious liberty lay in emigration to tolerant Pennsylvania.

Bearing a bitter grudge against England and the established church, Presbyterian Scots came in droves to America, entering chiefly at the the port of Philadelphia, though some landed at Charleston, New York, Boston, and other ports. They were a poor but determined people. Finding the tidewater region already preempted, they pushed into the hinterland, past even the Germans who had preceded them, and settled on the most distant frontiers. From Pennsylvania they pushed down the Cumberland Valley into Maryland and Virginia. Eventually they made their way into the hill country of the Carolinas, where they met some of their brethren who had moved inland from Charleston and Wilmington. Before 1750, Germans, Scots, and a sprinkling of tidewater Virginians had settled the Shenandoah Valley of Virginia. The Scots, however, soon were the dominant influence in the Shenandoah and other inland valleys, and the Presbyterian Church was the dominant religion of the western frontier.

While Scots and Germans were percolating into the frontier regions of the central and southern colonies and occupying such land as seemed good to them, speculation in vast territories in the West was beginning to excite the gambling instincts of men on both sides of the Atlantic. The second William Byrd, who had led the surveying party that ran the dividing line between Virginia and North Carolina in 1728, realized the value of frontier land and made haste to capitalize upon the wave of speculation that was already beginning. He bought 20,000 acres at the confluence of the Dan and Irvine rivers on the North Carolina frontier and later added another 6,000 acres which he hopefully named the Land of Eden. In 1642 he acquired 105,000 additional acres on the frontier, and by the time of his death in 1744 his land totaled 179,440 acres.[28] To find settlers for this great barony, Byrd supplied a Swiss land agent with notes for a promotional tract, published in Switzerland in 1737 as *Neu-gefundenes Eden* (New Found Eden). The tempting description of this paradise in the wilds of North Carolina and Virginia actually persuaded a shipload of Swiss to embark, but they were wrecked in sight of the promised land and only a few survivors reached shore. Byrd was at last reduced to selling land to Scots, who, he once complained, swarmed over the country like Goths and Vandals.

By the middle of the eighteenth century, the tide of land speculation was running high, and many investors were dreaming of Edens in the West greater than Byrd's barony. Thomas Lee, a prominent Virginian and president of the Virginia Council of State, organized in 1747 one of the most famous of the colonial land syndicates, known as the Ohio Company.[29] Its avowed purpose was the development of trade with the Indians in the West, the acquisition of land, and the establishment of white settlements in the region beyond the mountains. The plan was approved by the Board of Trade in London and by the governor and council in Virginia, subject to the erection of a fort at the forks of the Ohio and the settlement in the region of a hundred families within the next seven years.

The vicissitudes of the Ohio Company and the organization of rival companies to speculate in western lands constitute a complicated story too long for the telling here.[30] It will suffice to say that few escaped the land fever, and many of the fathers of the country, including George Washington, were deeply involved in speculation. Western lands were a potent factor in politics from this time onward.

When the Peace of Paris in 1763 at last ended the French and Indian War, colonial speculators once more dreamed of rich territories beyond the mountains, now happily free from invasion by the Canadian French. But the economic planners in London thought otherwise. They contemplated the revenue accruing from the fur trade with the western Indians and made plans to protect it. King George proclaimed that henceforth the English would not encroach upon the lands of the Indians west of the Appalachians, nor would settlers occupy territory there without the consent of the Indians. And with a stroke of the pen the Board of Trade drew a line along the crest of the mountains beyond which white emigrants were not to penetrate. The Proclamation Line of 1763 irritated but did not deter westward migration. The Board of Trade could no more stem the tide of westward migration with an imaginary line than King Canute could sweep back the sea with a broom.

The dream of new Edens in the West and of greater prosperity beyond the frontier line, wherever it was at any particular time, became the motivating influence upon thousands of Americans in the late colonial period and for the generations that followed. During the nineteenth century, migrants to the West saw in desolate swamps and deserts gardens that bloomed in their imaginations. Charles Dickens in *Martin Chuzzlewit* might satirize these American Edens, but frequently the dreams of the emigrants eventually came true. The Mormons in Utah had an Old Testament vision of an earthly paradise and by their own exertions achieved it. Innumerable migrants to California, from the Gold Rush onward, sought El Dorado or Eden—and in some fashion many of them found what they sought. Not even yet have we given up our dream of prosperity and the search for El Dorado. If we no longer have new lands to the west to tempt us, we have other frontiers of scientific discovery holding out the same promise that the new world offered to our ancestors. We are still searching for a terrestrial paradise, and perhaps some dreamers are already thinking of such discoveries in outer space. We are a restless people, and who knows what lies before us?

Notes

1. Various revisionists have recently attempted to show the beneficence of the Navigation Acts. See Lawrence P. Gipson, *The Coming of the Revolution, 1763–1775.* The New American Nation Series (New York, 1954), p. 25.

2. Quoted by James E. Gillespie, *The Influence of Oversea Expansion on England to 1700* (New York, 1920), p. 48.

3. Charles M. Andrews, *The Colonial Period of American History* (New Haven, Conn., 1936), II, 240–73. Andrews gives a detailed account of the early struggles for control of Barbados and the gradual emergence of the island as a crown colony fitting into the mercantilist scheme of things. During the quasi-independent period of the island's existence, much of its prosperity had come from its freedom to trade with the Dutch.

4. Gillespie, *Influence of Oversea Expansion,* p. 120.

5. *Ibid.,* p. 73.

6. Gipson, *Coming of the Revolution,* pp. 13–14.

7. *Ibid.,* p. 15.

8. *Ibid.,* p. 16–17.

9. Susan Myra Kingsbury, *The Records of the Virginia Company of London* (Washington, D.C., 1933), III, 457.

10. Woodrow Borah, *Silk-Raising in Colonial Mexico* (Berkeley, Calif., 1943), p. 4.

11. *American Husbandry* (1775), edited by Harry J. Carman (New York, 1939), p. 356.

12. E. Merton Coulter, *Georgia, A Short History* (Chapel Hill, N.C., 1947), p. 58.

13. Louis B. Wright, *The Atlantic Frontier* (New York, 1951), p. 296.

14. *American Husbandry,* pp. 126–27.

15. *Ibid.,* p. 191.

16. *Ibid.,* pp. 353–54.

17. *Ibid.,* pp. 310–11.

18. *Ibid.,* p. 366.

19. This topic is discussed in Louis B. Wright, *The Colonial Search for a Southern Eden* (University, Ala., 1953), pp. 53 ff.

20. Montgomery's tract, edited by J. Max Patrick, has been reprinted in Emory University Publications, Sources and Reprints, Series IV (Atlanta, 1948).

21. Verner W. Crane, *The Southern Frontier, 1670–1732* (Durham, N.C., 1928), p. 280.

22. George H. Williams, *Wilderness and Paradise in Christian Thought* (New York, 1962), pp. 98 ff.

23. Clarence W. Alvord and Lee Bidgood, *The First Explorations of the Trans-Allegheny Region by the Virginians, 1650–1674* (Cleveland, 1912), pp. 112–13. See Louis B. Wright, "The Westward Advance of the Atlantic Frontier," *Huntington Library Quarterly,* XI (1948), 261–75. A few paragraphs included here are adapted from this essay.

24. Alvord and Bidgood, *First Explorations,* pp. 192–93.

25. *Ibid.,* p. 192.

26. *Memoirs of a Huguenot Family,* edited by Ann Maury (New York, 1872), pp. 287–89.

27. Hugh Jones, *The Present State of Virginia* (London, 1724), p. 14.

28. See "The Life of William Byrd, 1674–1744," in *The London Diary,* edited by Louis B. Wright and Marion Tinling (New York, 1958), pp. 41–42.

29. Thomas Perkins Abernethy, *Western Lands and the American Revolution* (New York, 1937), p. 5.

30. A detailed account of the Ohio and other companies is given by Abernethy, *Western Lands, passim.* See also Alfred P. James, *The Ohio Company, Its Inner History* (Pittsburgh, Pa., 1959), *passim.*

Index

Index

Account of Elysaeus, 7
Adam, 14
Africa, 2–3, 12, 13, 23–24, 31
Amadas, Philip, 15
Ambrose, St., 5
American Husbandry, 77; quoted, 74, 75–76
Asia, 2, 3, 4, 14, 44
Ayllón, Lúcas Vásquez de, 71

Bahamas, the, 4
Balboa, Vasco Núñez de, quoted, 10–11
Barbados, 66–67
Barlow, Arthur, 15
Batts, Capt. Thomas, 81–82
Bede, the Venerable, 5
Bermuda, 15, 56
Beverley, Robert, 82; *History and Present State of Virginia,* 56
Bezoar stone, 41, 48
Bimini, fabled island of, 9
Bland, Edward, 80–81; *The Discovery of New Britain,* quoted, 81
Board of Trade and Plantations. *See* Lords of Trade, London.
Bonoeil, John, treatise on silkworms, 34, 35
Brazil, 23
Bright, Timothy, *A Treatise . . . of English Medicines,* 43
Byrd, William, I, 81–82
Byrd, William, II, 15, 86; *Neugefundenes Eden* (New Found Eden), 15, 86; treatise on plague, 58

Ça da Mosto, Alvise, 3
California, 88
Canada, 30, 67, 87
Cape of Good Hope, circumnavigated, 3
Casas, Bartolomé de las, 24
Cattle raising, 24, 29, 32, 84
Cecil, Sir Robert, 13
Charles VIII, King of France, 3
China (Cathay), 2, 3, 8, 21, 22
China smilax, 45, 46
Chute, Anthony, *Tobacco,* 50–51

Clayton, the Rev. John, 82
Clifford, George, third Earl of Cumberland, 12
Cochineal, 12, 31, 77, 78
Columbus, Christopher, 3–6, 7, 8, 9, 12, 44, 48; quoted, 5–6
Cortez, Hernando, 11
Coxe, Dr. Daniel, 82
Crusaders' reports of Eastern products, 2
Cuba, 4, 9, 48
Cuming, Sir Alexander, 78–79

Dias, Bartholomew, 3
Diaz de Isla, Dr. Ruy, *Tractado contra el mal serpentino,* 44
Dickens, Charles, *Martin Chuzzlewit,* 87
Dickson, Sarah Augusta, *Panacea or Precious Bane,* quoted, 52
Discourse concerning the Plague, A, quoted, 58–59
Drake, Sir Francis, 12, 54, 55
Drugs. *See* Medicines.
Duns, Joannes, Scotus, 5
Dyer, Sir Edward, 27, 42, 43
Dyestuffs, 22, 23, 25, 31, 65. *See also* Cochineal; Indigo.

East Indies, 23
Eden, Garden of, 7, 14, 28. *See also* paradise, earthly.
Eden, Land of, 15, 86
Egmont, John Perceval, first Earl of, 73
El Dorado, legend of, 16, 88
Elizabeth I, Queen of England, 12, 16, 25, 50, 53
Estienne, Charles and Liebault, Jean, *L'Agriculture et maison rustique,* 50
Eton, tobacco at, 51–52
Eve, 7

Fallam, Robert, 81–82; journal, 81, quoted, 82
Ferdinand, King of Spain, 4, 5, 10, 11
Fishing industry, 27–29, 36–38, 67, 69
Florida, 8–10, 24, 77, 79
Fontaine, John, journal, 82–83, quoted, 83

Fountain of youth, 7, 8–10, 41
Frampton, John, *Joyful News,* 42, 43, 44, 45–46, 48, 49, quoted, 42–43, 46
France, 12, 22, 23, 28, 37, 38, 39, 44, 49, 50, 64
Frobisher, Martin, 21–22
Furs, 31, 36–37, 38, 81

Gama, Vasco da, 3
Gates, Sir Thomas, 15
Genoa, 2
George I, King of England, 87
Georgia, 72–73, 74–76, 78
German immigrants, 84–85, 86
Gilbert, Sir Humphrey, 27, 30
Gilbert, Raleigh, 37
Gold, 3, 4–5, 6, 7, 9, 10–11, 12–13, 14, 16–17, 21–22, 23, 24, 37, 56, 68, 71
Gosnold, Bartholomew, 37
Guaiacum (*lignum vitae*), 45
Guiana, 16–17, 18

H., I., *Work for Chimney Sweeps,* quoted, 52–53
Hakluyt, Richard, the elder, 25–26, 27, 29, 30–32, 33, 39, 42; "Inducements" (1585), 30, quoted, 31–32; "Inducements" (n. d.), quoted, 32; "Notes," quoted, 26
Hakluyt, Richard, the younger, 23, 25, 26, 30; *A Discourse of Western Planting,* 25; *Divers Voyages,* 26
Harriot, Thomas, 54; *A Brief and True Report,* quoted, 54, 55
Harvey, Dr. Gideon, *A Discourse of the Plague,* 52
Hawkins, Sir John, 12, 23–24, 27, 50
Hawkins, William, 23
Hearne, Thomas, cited, 51–52
Henry VII, King of England, 3
Henry VIII, King of England, 23
Henry, Prince, the Navigator, 2
Hojeda, Alonso de, 8
Howes, Edmund, *Annals,* quoted, 50
Huon of Bordeaux, 7

India, 3, 7, 8, 23
Indians, new world, carried to Europe, 37, 44, 79; conversion urged, 81; slavery, 24, 71–72; trade, 31, 36, 37, 81–82, 84, 86, 87; treaties, 85, 87; use of tobacco, 48, 49, 54–55
Indigo, 76
Iron mining, 29, 68–69
Isabella, Queen of Spain, 4, 5
Isidore, St., 5

Italy, 22, 32, 33. *See also* Genoa; Naples; Venice.
Iter ad Paradisum, 7

James I, King of England, 16, 33–35, 36, 39, 70; *Counterblast to Tobacco,* 34, quoted, 53; *His Majesty's Gracious Letter,* quoted, 34
Jamestown, 15, 22, 33, 35, 47, 55, 56, 70, 71, 82
Jews, European, Cuming's colonization plan, 78–79
John II, King of Portugal, 3
Johnson, Sir Nathaniel, 72
Jones, Hugh, *Present State of Virginia,* quoted, 83

Kemp, William, *A Brief Treatise . . . of the Pestilence,* 51, 52

Land speculation, 78–81, 82–83, 87
Lane, Ralph, letter quoted, 32, 33
Lee, Thomas, 86
Legend of Seth, 7
Liebault, Jean and Estienne, Charles, *L'Agriculture et maison rustique,* 50
L'Obel, Matthias de, *Stirpium adversaria nova,* 50
Lok, Michael, 21
Lords of Trade, London, 39, 63–64, 65, 68, 70, 72, 76, 82, 86, 87

"Madre de Dios," 12–13
Magellan, Ferdinand, 2–3
Maine, 36, 37
Mandeville, Sir John, 17
Maneo, 16
Martyr, Peter, 9, 10, 12, quoted, 9–10; *Decades of the New World,* quoted, 9
Maryland, 57, 65, 85
Massachusetts Bay colony, 83
Medicines, 7–8, 22, 32, 41–55, 58–61, 66
Menzies, Archibald, 79
Mercantilism, 22, 25–26, 27–39, 63–79 *passim*
Mexico, 11, 21, 42, 71–72
Molasses, 66, 67
Monardes, Nicolás, 42, 43; *Dos libros,* cited, 44–46, 47–49, quoted, 42, 46, 49
Montezuma, King of Aztecs, 11
Montgomery, Sir Robert, *A Discourse of a New Colony,* quoted, 78
Morison, Samuel Eliot, quoted, 8

Naples, 44
Navigation Acts, 64, 69

Navy, English, growth of, 29, 31–32
Netherlands, the, 23, 37–38, 58, 64
New England, 37–38, 67–68, 69–70
Newfoundland, 27–30, 38, 64, 69
Newport, Capt. Christopher, 47
Nicot, John, 49
Nicotiana rustica, 55
Nicotiana tabacum, 55
Niño, Peralonso, 8
North Carolina, 13, 15, 30, 75, 81
Northwest passage, 14, 21, 22, 82
Nuce, Capt. Thomas, letter quoted, 70–71

Oglethorpe, Gen. James, 73, 78
Ohio Company, 86–87
Olive oil, 25, 26, 31, 42, 73, 78, 79
Oviedo y Valdez, Gonzalo Fernández de, 42

Panama, Isthmus of, 10
Paracelsus, Theophrastus Bombastus von Hohenheim, 43
Paradise, earthly, 4–18 *passim,* 25, 80, 81, 87–88
Paria, Gulf of, 5, 8
Parkhurst, Anthony, 27, 30; letter quoted, 27–28, 29, 30
Pastorius, Francis Daniel, 84
Peace of Paris (*1763*), 87
Pearls, 4, 6, 8, 10, 11, 13, 14
Penn, William, 84, 85
Pennsylvania, 74, 83, 84–85
Peru, 11, 16–17
Philip II, King of Spain, 25
Pizarro, Francisco, 11
Plague, 51–52, 58–59
Platter, Thomas, quoted, 53
Polo, Marco, *Travels,* 3, 6
Ponce de León, Juan, 8–10, 41
Popham, George, 37
Portugal, 2–4, 12, 23, 31, 32, 37, 49, 50
Prester, John, 3
Pring, Martin, 37
Proclamation Line of *1763,* 87
Propaganda for colonization, 84–86
Puerto Rico, 9
Puritans, American, 80, 83–84

Raleigh, Sir Walter, 7, 12, 13–14, 15–18, 25, 54; *History of the World,* 81, quoted, 13–14; *The Discoverie of . . . Guiana,* quoted, 16–17
Rice, 73, 76
Rolfe, John, 55
Ross, Alexander, *The Marrow of History,* 81, quoted, 13–14

Royal African Company, 24
Royal Society of London, 58, 82
Rum, 66, 67, 68

Sandys, Sir Edwin, 70
Sarsaparilla, 45–46
Sassafras, 45–47, 54, 61
Scotch-Irish immigrants, 84, 85–86
Shakespeare, William, *Othello,* quoted, 17
Shipbuilding industry, 67, 69
Silk, 2, 12, 22, 31, 32, 33–36, 39, 64, 65, 70–76, 78
Silver, 2, 11, 37
Slave labor, 24, 65, 66–67, 71
Slave trade, 9, 23, 24, 67–68
Smith, Capt. John, 36–38; *The Description of New England,* 36, quoted, 37, 38
Southampton, Henry Wriothesley, third Earl of, 34; letter quoted, 35
South Carolina, 14, 67, 72, 75, 76, 79, 84
South Sea Company, 77
Spain, 28, 29, 31, 32–33; in new world, 4, 8, 10, 11–12, 16, 21, 23–24, 25; trade, 4, 12, 22, 25–26, 33, 37, 39, 42–43, 52, 64; use of tobacco, 48, 50, 55; war with England, 33
Sparke, John, 24
Spices, 2, 7–8, 12, 13, 41, 82
Spotswood, Gov. Alexander, 82–83
Steel industry, 68–69
Stow, John, Annals, 50
Strabo, 5
Sugar, 23, 31, 64, 65–68
Syphilis, 44–45

Test Act of *1704,* 85
Thorius, Dr. Raphael, *Hymnus tabaci,* 51
Tobacco, condemned by King James, 33–36, 53; cultivation, 55, 56, 65, 66, 67, 76; financial value, 36, 52, 54, 55–58, 64, 65; medicinal value, 48–49, 50–52, 54–55, 58–60; use of, Europeans, 49, 50, 53–54, 55, 58–59, Indians, 48, 49, 54, 55
Toscanelli, Paolo del Pozzo, 3
Trade, Colonial, 63–64, 67–68, 69–70, 81–82, 84; Eastern, 1–4, 41; English, with colonies, 56, 57, 64, 65–67, 68–69, 76, with Europe, 21, 25, 26, 31, 32, 39, 56, with New Spain and Africa, 23, 24, 77; European, 21–22
Turnbull, Dr. Andrew, 79

Utah, 87

Venezuela, 5, 8, 10

Venice, 2, 4

Virginia, 58; commodities, 32–36, 55–57, 65, 66, 75; Council of, 47, 86–87; settlement, 15, 30, 80–83, 85–86

Virginia Company of London, 34, 35, 47, 70

Walsingham, Sir Thomas, 25

Washington, George, 87

West Indies, 24, 42, 44, 64, 65–67

Westward expansion, 65, 79–88

Weymouth, George, 37

Williams, Roger, 83

Wine, 6, 25, 26, 31, 33–36, 64, 65, 73, 74, 75–76, 77, 78

Wood, Abraham, 80–81, 81–82

Wood, Thomas, 81–82